Looking at Language in the Primary School

Edited by
COLIN MILLS
and
LINNEA TIMSON

The National Association
for the Teaching of English

First published: November 1988
Reprinted: November 1989, 1991 and 1992

ISBN: 0 901291 10 2

Published by:
The National Association for the Teaching of English
Birley School Annexe, Fox Lane, Frecheville, Sheffield S12 4WY

© NATE 1988

Printed in England by Short Run Press Ltd, Exeter

Looking at Language in the Primary School

WITHDRAWN

Books are to be returned on or before
the last d

NATE 0-11 Committee and Working Party

Linda Ashworth *Clifford Bridge School, Coventry*
Anne Baker *Courthouse Green Primary School, Coventry*
Gail Bedford *Mount Pleasant Primary School, Dudley*
Angela Exley *Sheffield LEA*
Carol Fox *Brighton Polytechnic*
Gillian Lathey *Advisory teacher, ILEA*
Colin Mills *University of Exeter*
Cliff Moon *Bulmershe College, Reading*
Shirley Paice *Epping County Infants School*
Deirdre Pettitt *University of Durham*
Sue Smedley *Lucas Vale Primary School, Deptford*
Sandra Smidt *William Patten Infants School, Hackney*
Anne Thomas *Centre for Language in Primary Education, ILEA*
David Thompson *Lingwood First School, Norwich*
Linnea Timson *College of St Mark and St John*

Contents

Teachers Looking . . .

The impetus for this collection came from members of NATE's 0-11 Committee. Over the last few years, each of us has been involved in bringing about change in the language and literacy policies of primary schools. We would like to think that our reflections upon what we have learned will help other teachers, and hope that the book will be a stimulus for discussion in staff meetings, school-based workshops and in-service courses. Although the articles have been written by individuals, they have been read and discussed by all the contributors. The 'talking points' or 'activities' which follow each piece reflect our discussions and provide possible starters for action amongst teachers.

We share some fundamental ideas. We view children as active and autonomous learners. Our understanding of the ways in which children learn their mother tongue convinces us that language is *acquired*, rather than being directly taught. Children learn to talk through interaction with parents, adults and other children, and we view this learning process as a powerful analogy for our understanding of how children learn to read and write. We see how these processes always occur in social and cultural contexts. Language and literacy learning is always meshed in with children's social identity, and with their feelings. You will meet dozens of children of these pages, from different cultures. We have tried to share the ways in which we have looked at them learning their language (sometimes, their second one) and learning to be literate.

That 'looking' leads us to another belief we all share. Reflecting upon what we have seen in our classrooms has led us towards deeper understandings of what we, and our colleagues, are about. Sometimes, that has involved changing our views and our practices. We have often been led to question the 'taken for granted', to make shaky our established wisdom. Margaret Donaldson, in *Children's Minds*, gets close to the process perhaps when she talks about 'heightening what is actual by considering what is possible'.

For example, when Sandra Smidt (in *Beginnings*) looks at Kahir's developing linguistic competence, and sees not a smooth progression, but undulating change, she questions long-cherished notions of 'development'. In her second contribution, she shows how her understanding of cultural diversity has been extended to enfold the experiences of a little girl, born in Hackney, writing stories about her mother's homeland.

When those outside schools and classrooms entreat us to quantify 'progress', it is timely that we, as teachers, articulate our emergent understandings as clearly as possible. These articles, together, show some of the kinds of evidence of children learning that we have seen in our classrooms. We hope that our readers will discuss (and argue with) our claims, and be encouraged to share their own experiences of children learning to talk, read and write.

A special mention must be made of a past member of the Committee, Linda Ashworth. The original proposal for the collection was hers, arising out of her work in developing a language policy. Her document, placed at the end of the collection, encapsulates in a single form many of the ideas which occur in individual articles.

Colin Mills

. . . into Partnership

Both Sandra Smidt and Anne Thomas, the writers in this first section, see the importance of partnership in learning. Partnership between child and child, child and adult, and home and school.

In *Beginnings*, starting with two stories involving children she knows, Sandra Smidt shows how close observation of one child's emergence as a confident talker, reader and writer reveals a new way of looking at 'progress' and 'development'. She outlines some of the ways in which our view of language acquisition and development has changed, and defines the role of supportive adults in aiding children's learning.

Anne Thomas develops and extends Sandra Smidt's claim that 'parents are experts in what their children already know when they start school'. Drawing on her own considerable experience, she provides a comprehensive framework of questions designed to help a staff promote these *connections* more effectively.

Beginnings

Gillian Lathey, Sandra Smidt, Viv Wilson

> What we need to do, and all we need to do, is bring as much of the world as we can into school and the classroom; give children as much help and guidance as they need and ask for; listen respectfully when they feel like talking; and then get out of the way. We can trust them to do the rest. (John Holt)

Two stories . . . Chizzy and Kahir:

Chizzy is four years old. Her parents are both teachers and she has had a lot of stories told and read to her from when she was very small. One day, on her way to school, her mother started talking about how, when she was at school, all the children had to wear a uniform. Chizzy was very interested in this and asked a lot of questions. The conversation lasted for a long time and, finally, she turned to her mother and said, in a perplexed voice, 'But I still don't understand. How did you get that bump on your head?'

It took some time for her mother to work out that Chizzy had understood the word 'unicorn' for the word 'uniform' and had tried, by questioning her mum, to make sense of what seemed to her like nonsense. She had, perhaps, heard a word which fitted in with her experiences and expectations and preoccupations and then tried to fit that to the answers to her questions.

Chizzy is not an exceptional little girl. Her serious, logical attempts to make sense of the situation are typical of the way in which most, if not all, children learn. Children live in a world filled with noise, music, oral language, visual information, smells, print, rules and other people. Out of all this seeming chaos they have to select those things they want to attend to; they have to organise what they see and hear and generalise from it. Children are constantly engaged, almost always through interaction with other people, in trying to make sense out of what they encounter. And they do this in a very logical and structured fashion, by making their own guesses or hypotheses about how things work, testing these out in real situations, generalising from these experiences and then making predictions or guesses about possible out-

10

comes.

Kahir is the fourth of five children. His parents came to London from Bangladesh when he was a baby. His older brother and sisters started school knowing no English and very confused by a new country, a new system and a new language. None of them went into a nursery class. When Kahir was three he was offered a place in the nursery. It was immediately apparent that he, like all his peers, had already learned a great deal. He could talk fluently and volubly in Bengali/Sylheti. He could dress and feed himself and go to the toilet. He could run and jump and climb and ride a tricycle. He also knew things like how to use a chapatti pan, the names of lots of different kinds of cars and how to bath a baby.

Kahir was lucky because one of the Nursery Assistants was a Bengali speaker. Kahir could communicate with her and she was able to find out from his family a lot about his early experiences and interests. His father worked in a restaurant and it soon became apparent that Kahir knew a lot about food and about money. At first he was quiet, observing, with bright eyes, what was going on around him. Often he would play on his own – very physical activities, calling out for praise 'Miss! Miss!' Then, slowly, he was drawn to quieter activities and would look at picture books and murmur aloud in Sylheti, or draw and paint, or play in the Home Corner, or listen to taped stories. As his confidence grew, so did his use of English. He started to re-tell stories and to put writing into his pictures.

When he was five Kahir moved into a vertically grouped class. His teacher was also a Bengali speaker. She watched him and saw his eagerness to continue learning and his pride in his grow-ing skills at drawing, writing and telling stories. Because she was aware of just how much he knew and, from her own experiences of learning a second language, of the struggle he had gone through, she kept on boosting his confidence. Her expectations of what he could achieve were high. At the same time he had other children in his class talking to him, helping him, showing him how to do things, admiring his beautiful drawings and raising his own expectations of what he could do.

At the end of his first year in the Infant school, he seemed to have reached a plateau. He spent much of his time making Lego models, playing in the sand and water, reading comfortingly familiar books. His teacher watched and waited. Then he made a spurt in number. He demanded pages of sums and started doing sums using Bengali number symbols. He also went to Bengali classes in school and started to write in Bengali.

Soon he was reading English quite fluently. The mistakes he made often indicated that much of his learning had come about from sitting on the fringes of groups, listening. He had learned a lot about decoding, and the errors he made often showed a lack of comprehension. His teacher started reading more and more to him. At this stage he became anxious about being correct, reluctant to take risks. His writing became repetitive, static and dependant on the teacher. But the school was trying to move children towards being more autonomous as writers and so his teacher encouraged him to take risks and not to worry about getting things wrong. Slowly he responded and, as he started to try and spell words on his own, for example, so he became more self-critical in a positive way. His parents do not read and write at home in English, but his older sister helps him and all the family are very interested in his success. At the end of his Infant schooling he took a leading part in a school show and performed confidently, enthusiastically and with a great sense of humour.

Kahir's father, when told of his achievements in school, said 'One day he will be an important man.'

Children learning . . .

The role of the child as learner has been under careful consideration since the early 1960s when the psycholinguists started analysing the acquisition of oral language. Until that time much of the research into the acquisition of spoken language had been in the behaviourist mode and had focused on looking at things like the number and range of words spoken by children at different ages. The underlying assumption was that children make a random sound, perhaps imitating the sounds they hear around them. Parents or other adults respond to this and children learn that this sound elicits this positive response. Or parents show children an object – say, a book – and, at the same time say the noun 'book'; this is repeated and repeated until the child makes the same sound in response to the same stimulus.

The model of the psycholinguists is both more dynamic and

more social. Children are no longer viewed as passive receivers of imparted information. Rather they are engaged in trying to understand the language surrounding them and, in trying to understand the language, they make hypotheses, formulate tentative rules and test predictions. Wells (1981) shows that children do not first acquire language and then use it. Children acquire language and use it at the same time to try and make sense of the world around them. They comment on things, ask questions, encounter problems and look for solutions, often enlisting the help of adults.

Since this early language acquisition usually takes place in the home, the relationship between child and parents is obviously a key factor. Wells observed that parents usually treat children as equal partners in dialogue, encouraging them to initiate discussion and being willing to follow the child's agenda rather than impose their own. This interaction is a reciprocal one and meanings are jointly negotiated rather than being unilaterally imposed.

Teachers learning . . .

If we have a model of the child in school continuing to learn in this way, what implications does it have for us, as teachers? We know that all children, coming to school for the first time, have, like Kahir, already learned a great deal. They have learned general things like how to feed and dress themselves, how to go to the toilet, how to run and jump. They have also learned things that are more 'culture' specific – perhaps how to put on a sari, or all about He-man and She-ra. It is important for us to know *what* children know and to use their knowledge as a basis to build on. With some children, perhaps those for whom English is a second language, this poses particular problems. But we do need to attend carefully to what children do and say in order to find out what they know. And, of course, we need to establish a dialogue with other family members to help us in this.

Parents are experts on what their children already know when they start school and on what their interests are out of school. Very often, however, parents are unaware of the significance of what they know and of its relation to formal schooling. So it is important that we set up non-threatening and non-judgmental situations with parents if we are to enlist their vital help and expertise.

When children first start school we must allow them time to look and listen. We need to bear in mind that, for children whose homes are close to the values and expectations of school, the adjustment to school is likely to be easier than for other children. We need to talk to children and to listen to them in order to find out what they know and what their interests are. We need to show them that we respect and acknowledge their language, their culture, their interests. In this way we can build on the confidence they bring with them. Most of us have encountered very young children who have a certainty about their abilities. They believe they can read and write; often it is the adults and other children who tell them they can't. These children are not deluded. They recognise the fact that their writing cannot be read by others and that their reading is not an exact interpretation of the text. But they have the confidence to 'have a go' and it is essential that this confidence is maintained. Anxiety is the biggest killer of learning.

When children are learning at home and encounter a problem they ask for help and usually get it. In schools we are more reluctant to help children, often directing them to a chart, a book or to some inner resources. There seems little reason for not helping a child when requested to do so. Why not spell a difficult word or show the child how to use a paintbrush? We can, of course, continue to encourage children to be autonomous and to take risks, but withholding help does seem to be taking things a little too far.

What about intervention? The child, prepared to have a go at finding out or doing for herself, should be allowed to continue. Any intervention on the part of the teacher should be sensitive and this sensitivity should be extended to the way in which we handle the errors children make. Errors often reveal the processes children are going through and give us some insight into the child's struggle to make sense of the world, like Chizzy's unicorn.

So we want children to be in charge of their own learning. An audience may or may not be appropriate. We want to offer children a wide choice of media for recording experiences, thoughts, emotions. If the child decides to do a painting, the painting should be primary and we should resist the temptation to ask the child to 'write about it'. If a story has been written and the child chooses to illustrate it, fine. If not, the medium of print was the one that was important for the child on that particular occasion. Of course we should continue to widen children's horizons and to offer them opportunities to attempt new and different approaches. We may suggest referring to information books or interviewing someone; we might encourage a scientific or mathematical approach to a problem. But these things will only have relevance for the child if the question to be answered arose in the child's mind.

The work that children produce – the product: painting, story, tape – is never an end in itself, but merely a step along the way to further learning. When children make several attempts at a drawing, for example, each one is a draft for the next. The child stops because she has no further question in her mind at that particular time. Keeping a child's work together in a folder of some sort creates a profile of the child's growth as a learner and provides child, parent and teacher with a valuable record of how skills, understanding and interests have developed over a period of time.

Children do not learn in a linear fashion, but rather in bursts with lulls which often mean a period of consolidation of what has been learned. Often the consequence of these lulls is a sudden burst in achievement and expression and the profile is a way of monitoring this and of showing parents that it is sometimes important for children to be given time to absorb knowledge and reflect on it. Lulls in apparent progress can, of course, be caused by emotional difficulties.

Children learn from other children and from adults. Donald Graves (1983) shows that children who share their writing with each other are amazingly sensitive, supportive and detailed in their questioning. The discussion sessions about one another's writing provide children with ideas and models while the interaction with their peers also encourages individual confidence. Adults also provide models for children and the child, as apprentice in the learning situation, should see that the adult model is not instant or magical, but rather involves the same sort of struggle that the child engages in. Children, shown the series of sketches an artist does before completing a picture, have a perfect view into the process, for example. We should immerse children in literature and poetry, in art and music. Through fantasy and symbolism they allow children to explore threatening feelings and hypothetical situations. (Linnea Timson takes up this theme in a later paper.)

Many of us are currently re-considering and re-evaluating our approaches to teaching and it seems essential to keep in mind a framework of the child as learner. The way in which we perceive the learning process will then inform our teaching. We are in a phase in education when more and more pressures are being brought for a return to what some people like to term 'basics' and, in order for us to defend our methods and the quality of education on offer to our children, it is crucial that we have a sound theoretical framework to build on.

*

TALKING POINTS AND ACTIVITY

Sandra Smidt's outline of Kahir's growth reveals a different model from that often given in accounts of 'language development'. Can you think of occasions when a child has reached a plateau, or even on the surface appears to be going backwards, yet is in fact consolidating his or her learning?

Consider keeping a folder of a child's work (drawing; talking and writing) over a period and through this profile attempt to understand the child's growth as a learner.

Throughout this book emphasis is placed on the central importance of children generating their own language learning. What kind of individual conversations and discussions could help you in promoting this? How could tape-recording a group of children working or a child discussing her work with you help?

Making Connections:
Children, Parents and Schools

Anne Thomas

It was common in the sixties and early seventies to disregard the essential part played by parents in the formal education of their children. The teaching of literacy was considered to be the responsibility of professional teachers in schools. Whatever parents may have thought was part of a necessary preparation was regarded either as inappropriate or in some instances counter-productive. Thus parents were not only discouraged from taking part in the school's literacy policy, that is from working alongside the teacher in support of current methodology, but were also forever being castigated for teaching their children to read using a variety of approaches or for teaching them to write through forming letters 'incorrectly'. This kind of interference, they were told, created confusion in the minds of the children and furthermore these 'bad habits' had to be consciously unlearned.

By the eighties research both here and abroad, and developing experiences in schools, has informed us better of how children learn. It is these findings that are worth considering when developing policy and implementing practice in primary schools. At the beginning of Chapter 7 in the Bullock Report (1975) there was evidence of uncertainty as to the role of the parent in helping the child to learn to read prior to starting school. The uncertainty arose from a confusion as to what was involved in learning. On the one hand the authors of the report were concerned with the mechanics of reading *per se* and on the other the pleasure that could accrue from reading familiar stories to the child on demand. It would be fair to say that this dilemma about reading pedagogy still persists in the minds of many educationalists.

Direct references, from the Bullock Report, which are open to different interpretation, read as follows:

> 7.1 A recurring topic of discussion, and one which often arouses much feeling, is the age at which children should actually begin the process of learning to read . . . the question is one of particular concern to parents . . . should they give any kind of reading instruction before the child starts

17

school? If not, how far should they be involved once the child has started school, and in what ways? Should it all be left to the teacher with no home involvement beyond general encouragement?

Let us make it clear at once that we believe parents have an important part to play.

7.2 It has been said that the best way to prepare the very young child for reading is to hold him on your lap and read aloud to him stories he likes, over and over again.

In 1976, Margaret Clark's book *Young Fluent Readers* was published. Her research findings gave much food for thought. Whereas the majority of research before then had focused on children with reading difficulties, Clark studied thirty-two children who were able to read before starting school at five. Furthermore, the children were not necessarily of outstanding ability, nor did they all come from professional backgrounds. The notable common factors, however, were the parents' prevailing interest in their respective children's learning, a natural desire to converse and to share books, and also the encouragement of autonomy in decision and choice. *Few parents had made any systematic attempt to teach reading.*

Gordon Wells (1982) noted that story-telling and story-reading play a crucial part in children's literacy development, particularly when the child is given time and space to interact with the text and when the constructing of meaning is central to the activity. A fine example of this kind of interaction is a mother's sharing of the book *The Giant Jam Sandwich* by John Vernon Lord, (Piccolo 1972), with her three-year-old son, David.

Notice how the mother leaves space for the child to offer his comments and how her contributions build on his, extending his understanding of both the matter of the story and the actual wording.

M: 'One hot summer in Itching Down [*M reads*]
Four millions wasps flew into town'

D: I don't like wasps . . .
    flying into town

M: Why's that?

D: Because they sting me

M: Do they?

D: Mm. I don't like them

M: They'll only sting you if they get angry
If you leave them alone they won't sting you

But four million would be rather a lot
   wouldn't it?
They'd get rather in the way
'They drove the picnickers away [*M reads*]

D: Mm

M: They chased the farmers from their hay
They stung Lord Swell (*chuckles*) on
   his fat bald –'

D: Pate

M: D'you know what a pate is?

D: What?

M: What d'you think it is?

D: Hair

M: Well – yes
It's where his hair SHOULD be
It's his head – look his BALD head
All his hair's gone

D: Where is it?

M: Well he's old so it's dropped out
He's gone bald

Wells 1982 p.186

In the work of Clark, Wells and in the study carried out by Jennie Ingham (1981) in two Bradford middle schools, another relevant and universal factor emerged: that of parental interest and, perhaps more importantly, the pleasure engendered through the sharing of stories and books with developing readers. There was striking evidence in the Bradford Book Flood Experiment showing that in the homes where parents were avid readers there was a distinct possibility that the children were also; similarly where parents were infrequent readers, so were the children. Evidence of this nature can create an aura of complacency, a belief that change is not a viable proposition. However, Jennie Ingham and others who have pursued research on similar topics were more positive in approach and demonstrated clearly that if teachers and parents were more involved as partners in children's reading, and more knowledgeable about children's books, the shared pleasure that accrued would enhance children's view of the activity.

There has been a substantial number of initiatives around the country where schools have involved parents in their children's education and in particular in shared-reading partnerships.[1] It is not appropriate to report on these in detail, but sufficient to say that the starting point for any initiative of this kind is to believe in and value the major contribution that parents and other experienced readers can make in furthering children's development. Research has shown, overwhelmingly, that *children learn first and foremost from their parents.* (Ferreiro and Teberosky (1983), Wells (1982), Widlake and MacLeod (1984).) Parents are interested in their children's progress. The difficulty lies in convincing some parents that they can play a crucial role in what is seen as the more professional aspects of the education system. In addition many teachers believe that parents are a threat to their professional expertise or they cite instances of apathy on the part of parents, who they say can never be contacted. So there exists in the minds of some parents and teachers alike a number of misunderstandings. Many of these misunderstandings are being resolved where PACT (Parents, Children and Teachers) schemes have been implemented. To say that any such schemes are not fraught with difficulties would be untrue and to agree with the methodology of some would go against the grain also. However, a great deal has been learnt from what has gone before and it is important to develop good practice based on this knowledge and experience.

Considerations and Suggestions for Developing a Policy:
Parents, Children and Teachers

There can be no prescriptive policy that would suit all schools; rather policies should be descriptive and be devised and continually developed for each particular school, bearing in mind the qualities and interests of members of staff, the needs of the children in the school and the willingness and availability of parents and other adults to support practice.

WHAT ARE THE MAJOR CONSIDERATIONS?
A. *Parents*
- How can a greater understanding between parents and teachers be established so that a genuine partnership is developed?
- What is going to be expected of parents in terms of knowledge of the teaching/learning of literacy?

20

- Are parents to be involved in school and at home?
- Does 'parental' support include other adults and older children who have regular contact with the child?
- How is contact going to be made with the parents initially?
- How can parents who are semi-literate or illiterate be helped to feel that they too can actively help?

B. *Children*
- How can a context be created whereby the children's view of literacy at home and at school are not in conflict?
- What strategies can be adopted to avoid putting any kind of undue pressure on children to 'succeed'?
- Is there a system of reading journals or logs so that children are equal contributors?
- In what ways are the needs and interests of bilingual children catered for?
- What about the children whose parents are unable, for a variety of reasons, to support the policy?
- In what ways might children's own stories be used as a natural reading resource for reading at home and at school?

C. *Teachers*
- How will teachers go about developing a policy based on a common understanding of what the school is trying to achieve for the children?
- Are all the teachers to be actively involved from the beginning; or will the scheme be established step by step?
- How will the scheme be appraised? What will count as evidence of success? How will the initial enthusiasm be sustained?
- How can it be ensured that the most important ingredient in such a policy is the enjoyment and pleasure that is gained from reading and writing?

D. *Organisation and Book Resources*
- How are parents to be introduced to the scheme? A whole school meeting; a series of workshops; as individuals over a period of time?
- Is the whole school to be involved from the inception?

- How will the arrangements vary according to the age of the children? Is it easier/more difficult to organise for four-year-olds or for eleven-year-olds?
- Will the school be open to parents so that they can support children's reading development in the classroom?
- Will there be opportunities for parents and teachers to meet in order to discuss new books?
- How often will the children take books home – every day, twice a week?
- What role are parents/other adults/siblings going to play at home? Are they simply going to hear children read aloud or will the scheme have a more global view and encourage parents to read to children; to share texts; and to talk about the content of books, their respective authors and illustrators?
- Where are all the books going to come from? What happens if books get lost? What kinds of books will be available for loan? Who will choose the books?
- Will zipped plastic bags or something similar be purchased as protection for the books when being carried to and from school?
- Will there be a school bookshop? Will it be jointly run by parents and teachers and in some cases children?
- How can the local library be involved?
- How can parents/adults be encouraged to visit the school to tell stories in a variety of languages and from a number of cultures? Can some of these stories be published?

Particular recommendations

This series of questions and considerations is not exhaustive but is intended to act as a starting point for discussion at whole school staff meetings. The policy that eventually evolves will be specific to individual schools.

It might prove worthwhile, however, if one or two particular recommendations were made:

1. If the purposes of such a policy are to:
   - enrich children's reading experiences;

– demonstrate that reading is both pleasurable and worth-while;

– build upon what children know and can do;

then it is important to be clear as to what kinds of books are going to be available and why?

Barrie Wade in his research, published as *Story at Home and at School*, stated:

> Since narrative is a crucial way in which young children organise their understanding of the world and the main mode in which they articulate their ideas, its role in thinking and thus in the teaching and learning of young children should not be under-estimated. (Wade 1984, p. 32)

and

> there is a need for a greater awareness of the role of story and narrative in thinking and learning – an awareness that is most effective when shared by the partners in learning, both parent and teacher. (*Ibid.*, p. 33).

Similarly Margaret Meek (1982) in her book *Learning to Read* exhorted parents to consider the possibilities that reading fiction offers children and then went on to provide encouragement for the parent of a special kind:

> . . . literacy doesn't begin and end in the official sphere of social contracts. It concerns us as people who create our culture, in all its variety and complexity. Good readers are more than successful print-scanners and retrievers of factual information. They find in books the depth and breadth of human experience . . . Readers are at home in the life of the mind; they live with ideas as well as events and facts. They understand a wider range of feelings by entering into those of other people . . . My main contention is that we must offer all our children the possibility of this kind of reading, right from the start. (Meek 1982, p. 17).

and in reference to the parents' role in this partnership she said:

> it is to encourage the child to believe that reading is a worthwhile and pleasurable thing to do, that literacy is within his grasp, and to provide the means for his enjoyment and success . . . As you read together, he will learn to read, and you will learn about reading . . . It involves entering into an equal partnership with the teachers in school and with the children themselves. No child learns to read by reading only in school; he also needs supported practice. (*Ibid.*, pp. 26-7).

2. Choice of books is important and ways of getting to know them are vital also. Here are a few ideas of where help can be found:

- Local library;
- Local bookshops;
- *The Signal Selection of Children's Books*;[2]
- *The Good Book Guide*;
- *Books for Keeps* (published six times a year);
- *Picture Books for Young People 9-13*;
- Teachers, parents and children's own knowledge of books;
- Local story-telling groups.

3. Parents can become anxious if they are expected to be teachers of reading: there prevails a kind of mystique about the whole affair. In preference institute the notion that learning to read involves:

- an awareness that reading is all about enjoyment;
- constructing meanings;
- the sharing of texts;
- the realisation that the inexperienced reader may re-tell the story from the pictures – this is a natural part of a reader's development;
- an understanding that approximation to the text is a natural development – accuracy comes later;
- sharing ideas and speculations;
- looking at and talking about illustrations;
- creating a bond of understanding with the author;
- predicting sequences and possible outcomes;
- making errors, we all learn by making them;
- reading is a problem-solving activity;
- reading favourite books over and over again.

4. Keeping records is something that concerns all educationalists, and there are as many ways of monitoring children's achievement as can be imagined. Many of these, however, when scrutinised, do little more than provide spaces for ticks beside books that children have read. On the other hand reading journals or logs and reading conferences can provide a great deal of

information about reading habits, reading development, likes and dislikes and can in particular afford the child the opportunity to be a critical and discerning reader. The significant factors to be considered seem to be:

- how can there be a viable and worthwhile system which involves the children's, teachers' and parents' views?
- how can it be operated so that no one feels it an onerous task?
- how soon can young children be involved in recording views of their own development as readers?
- what can teachers learn about children's continuous development from a reading journal?
- what will be included and seen as valuable?

Here is an example of a page from a child's journal:

Name of Book	Date	Comments
Peace At Last by Jill Murphy	1.3.85 Parent	This is the third time she has brought this book home. She never tires of it, even if I do!
	2.3.85 Teacher	Have you noticed how she is wanting to read more of the story for herself?
	2.3.85 Child	I like this book.

Co-operation between parents and teachers in children's learning is a comparatively new field, although the research findings and examples of good practice are accumulating. The one clear direction in which such co-operation does take us is away from the traditional split between home and school and towards a genuine sharing of responsibility for children's education. We believe that this could signal a real turning-point for children and their learning ... Whatever the future holds, we are now convinced that parents must be included as partners in their children's learning. (Griffiths and Hamilton, 1984 p. 126)

1. Key Studies of Parental Involvement

CUES (Centre for Urban and Educational Studies) ILEA
Vauxhall Manor Building

Lawn Lane, London, SW8 1TU
Research Project: Family Co-operation in the Development of Literacy

PITFIELD PROJECT: (Hackney Teachers Centre ILEA)
Queensbridge School Building
Albion Drive, London, E8 4ET

TIZARD, J., SCHOFIELD, W. N. and HEWISON, J., (1982)
'Collaboration between teachers and parents in assisting children's reading', *British Journal of Educational Psychology* 52(1), 1-15.

COMMUNITY EDUCATION DEVELOPMENT CENTRE,
Lyng Hall, Blackberry Lane, Coventry, CV2 3JS
WIDLAKE, PAUL and MacLEOD, FIONA (1984)
Raising Standards: Parental Involvement Programmes and Language Performance of Children

2. Reviews of Children's Books

Sources of Information on Children's Books (ILEA)
Revised Edition 1987
A 46-page booklet which lists reviewing journals and periodicals and organisations which either give information or publish booklists or both. There are sections on book exhibitions and specialist London bookshops.
Centre for Language in Primary Education
Webber Row, London SE1 8QW

*

TALKING POINTS

Which of the recommendations made in this article seem particularly relevant to your school?

Bearing in mind the social context, and current preoccupations in your school, are there other recommendations you would add that would enable you to make 'connections'?

. . . into Classrooms

The next two articles take us into infant classrooms. They give us examples of new ways of looking at processes we often take for granted: children talking and children learning to read.

Deirdre Pettitt reminds us of the power of talk as a tool which 'we all use to refine our concepts and attitudes'. She shares some rich examples of children using talk to acquire new understandings and enter new modes of thinking in Mathematics. She then suggests ways in which we might revalue talk as a path for children into composing and writing.

Henrietta Dombey takes us into a classroom in which children learn to read 'for real' from the start. Just as the first article presents a view of children talking together as 'shared sense making', so we see the novice readers in the second come to know literacy as 'shared story making'. Reading is a social process from the beginning. Moreover, the article asserts the value of real texts which confer 'a sense of power on the apprentice readers'.

Significantly both writers tell us 'stories' about their classroom observations, and make theories from them: a model for what we could all do in sharing what we know with our colleagues?

Talking in Classrooms

Deirdre Pettitt

Voices

Talking with young children and listening carefully to what they say to you or to each other is a fascinating experience. In school it can indicate their cool common sense:

> Jamie (age 7)   So I stayed up to watch this video, right, and there was this thing and it was killing all these people and there were these heads and all the blood and that.
>
> Teacher   What happened?
>
> Jamie   I dunno it was boring. I went to bed.

What they say can lighten our day although it is tasteless and demoralising to laugh at children trying to make sense of the world through their talk. This fact seems to have escaped some television producers. However, a staffroom enjoyed one mother's predicament:

> Teacher   How is your [pregnant] mum?
>
> Sally (age 6)   Well alright but she had to go for an Xray. They thought she was going to have giblets.

Or the talk can be salutory. If the home corner is currently a school, listen with horror to your own teacherese:

> Annie (age 5)   Right, let's start. Oh dear what have I done with my glasses?
>
> Sue (age 5)   I can't hear what ANYONE says if you all talk at once.

All these voices are worth listening to. If a classroom has a tradition that everyone in it values what others have to say we don't have to teach children listening skills. The teacher listens to children and they listen to her and to each other. Of course, they switch off if there doesn't seem to be anything worth listening to or if, like everyone else, they want to retreat into their private world for a bit of peace and quiet. It is easy to sympathise with the child who said wistfully, when urged to leave an absorbing face paint he was designing for Ecuadorian Indians and change for P.E. 'What I'd really, really like to do is go in the quiet room and just sit.'

Talking at school and at home

Just sitting may not be high on our list of priorities for children but we might consider whether we do make provision for places where they can read or write quietly or simply re-charge their batteries. At other times they will want to talk. Then our serious purpose is *to foster the learning that takes place through talking.* This does not make our job any easier. If we had a class where children were told what to do they would fill in the boxes and colour the worksheets with good grace. Talk would go on but its character would be different from that in a classroom where children are encouraged to work out the problems to be solved with the teacher. In such classrooms children's eternal questions stretch teachers to their limits and land them in deep water as in Jane's question: 'I don't believe in God and Jesus and all that rubbish. Do you?' Jane was 7. Justin at 6 was rather easier to reply to but he was clearly extending his concepts and vocabulary: 'What do you call those ghosts what throw things about?' Unfortunately children do not always help us in our public relations. They are only too prone to go home after a golden day where we feel sure that conversation has enabled learning to take place and say (and I quote): 'We had a lovely day today. We didn't do anything!'

This is all the more unfortunate because there is considerable evidence *both that children are very good at learning through conversation and that homes facilitate this through the interaction that parents have with their children.* (Tizard and Hughes 1984) So we have to convince parents who are naturally worried about their children's progress that learning in school is not just a matter of getting right answers or copying neatly. We need to communicate that what we are doing is continuing the learning process

29

started at home. We are providing opportunities for talk, which is one of the things they did when they supplied the supportive context in which their children learned their mother tongue. We have to point out that conversation is a powerful way to learn. After all their children came to school with a huge amount of learning about language. They had learned many of the rules which make language work, had an extensive vocabulary and had the ability to use this knowledge to communicate success-fully. (Wells 1987) We build on this.

In many ways it is easier for parents than for us to teach children to learn through talk. They know the children and their past and future. They have a close intimate relationship with them and, crucially, they have fewer children to talk with. But over the years schools have worked out their own strategies assisted by such researchers as those mentioned above. Some-times we have concentrated too much on the rules and not enough on the interactions. As we were reminded several years ago:

> It might be a fruitful step for nursery school teachers to forget for a while about promoting language development, a process we do not under-standing sufficiently to prescribe for, and turn their attention instead to developing a wide range of joint activities with children in which language will naturally occur. (Tizard 1975)

We know a little more now but this advice is still sound and not only for nursery school teachers.

We have worked out various patterns of interaction in school. It seems likely that although the whole class meeting has its uses it is not a particularly good vehicle for productive learning through talk. A discussion demands a smaller group where all the partici-pants including the teacher have a role. Although the teacher's presence, as a skilled conversationalist, may push a conversation along most fruitfully, she cannot be everywhere at once. Parents can be invaluable helpers here. Tasks such as sewing, which are relatively undemanding, are often rich in conversation as children relax and feel able to initiate talk about anything under the sun which occurs to them. It has been noticed that some of the more demanding or creative tasks such as painting seem to be enjoyed in silence and there is a place for this also.

When children are working together without an adult they can learn from each other. A good deal of the conversation will be gossip but that can also involve learning. A lot of talk will be at the level of 'pass the rubber', but if the activity the children are doing is interesting and particularly if it demands debate and problem solving, talking is likely to be constructive. For instance, five-year-old children were observed to wrangle amicably for fifteen minutes when asked to arrange their own houses, trees, people and other pictures on a class frieze. Children who are writing together share ideas, completed stories and the more mundane problems such as spelling.

Very young children often indulge in monologues, occasionally and then more frequently involving their peers. These tell us a lot about what they are learning.

> Sarah (age 4)   (*exploring coloured water*)
> It's blue. Look it's blue. If I put this (a rag dyed blue by water) in the bucket it's purple. What colour is water? Your fingers are blue Jason. (*Sings*) Red and yellow and pink and blue . . .

Working together, children can be incredibly patient in the teaching role. The transcript from which the following excerpt has been taken has been cut because it was very, very repetitive. It involved a lot of saying numbers and counting but principally it involved one child patiently and seriously trying to instruct another by going over and over the same ground. Playing a mathematics game, Terry threw two dice. One showed zero the other two. The following exchange resulted:

Darren (age 7)	You've got two Terry.
Terry (age 7)	Two? It's not two.
Darren	Yeh. One, two. (*counts and points*)
Terry	No it's not. It must be twelve then.
Darren	No two.
Terry	That's twelve.
Darren	No look you have two and zero. That means you go two (*indicates two spaces on the board*)
Terry	Go there then?
Darren	No you have to go one two.

This went on for several more turns. Darren used a mixture of explanation and demonstration which finally convinced Terry, for the time being at least, that two and zero are two. Importantly however there was no sign of impatience or strain on either child.

Talking individually with children

It has to be admitted that it is likely that a teacher can be of most use to children when she is able to talk with just one. Of interest to teachers are the descriptions of passages of 'intellectual search' described by Tizard and Hughes (1984). These were extended one to one conversations between pre-school children and a parent where the former pursued a topic to some depth and refined their thinking. The adult role was to follow the children's lead and to enable them to ask questions and form hypotheses by encouragement and interest rather than any attempt to instruct. Opportunities for this sort of interaction are hard to make in school. When we can do this it may be well worth the effort as in the following example. John (age 6) was adding various numbers on to 10: $10+6$, $10+8$, $10+2$ and so on.

John	(*looking at 10+4*)
	1,2,3,4,5,6,7,8,9,10,11,13,14.
Teacher	Do you need to count to ten first?
John	Oh no – 11,12,13,14.
Teacher	That's good. Can you do 10+6?
John	Yes. 11,12,13,14,15,16.
Teacher	Mm can you do that one?
John	Yes but –
Teacher	Go on.
John	I wonder –
Teacher	What do you wonder?
John	If I started with that one (*points to 6*) and added that one (*points to 10*) would I still get 16?
Teacher	Well try it and see.
John	7,8,9,10,11,12,13,14,15,16, (*triumphant*) Yes I do.
Teacher	That's great. Try the others . . .

John's teacher resisted the temptation to leap in too quickly. She gave him a little time and listened. John made a significant step forward in understanding a mathematical concept.

The selection of an example from mathematical thinking is deliberate. Wells (1981) argued that language is most central at the 'creative' end of the curriculum and less so at the 'skills' end. He cited mathematics as an example of an area where closed questioning is often appropriate. However, language which allows children to demonstrate their thinking must be central to any area of the curriculum and mathematics involves invention, even if this is of known facts. John re-invented something that is known but he did it for himself. In any problem solving activity children may not be able to talk about what they can do without help. Teachers can say 'show me' before they help the child to put it into words. When we do ask children to show us or tell us what they have done they can surprise us. Often their methods are at least as good as the procedures we had in mind. They often, for instance, add the three numbers if required to multiply by three. This demonstrates that they know that one way of looking at multiplication is continuous addition. With a little help from a teacher children can make their own inventions. For example, Janey invented counting on over ten. She was reciting all the sums she could do within ten using her fingers to count:

Teacher	I bet you can't do 10+3.
Janey	(*looking horrified*) What in my head?
Teacher	Mm
Janey	(*counting all her fingers*) 1,2,3,4,5,6,7,8,9,10. (*spreads our her fingers and looks at them for a long interval*) I know. I know – 11,12,13.

Talking and Literacy

A major opportunity for one to one conversation is described in the next article. That is when children share their books with the teacher. Henrietta Dombey writes of a class of children who know they can read. They also know that sharing books is a social activity and another time when we talk together. Later on, when children read fluently, there is little point in simply hearing them read. The alternative of a reading conference is an occasion children value as their time with the teacher. It not only provides personal discussion about their interests in books and reading but gives them a private opportunity to talk with the teacher about other matters. A shy child may well use this time to seek re-assurance or raise questions. With any child the teacher can use the time to listen, to talk and to extend the conversation by her genuine interest in what is said.

Teachers' collaboration with young writers is also an example of learning through talk. Talking about writing needs to be the sensitive intervention of one writer suggesting ways forward to another. In this way it does not interfere with children's ideas and intentions. We all have difficulty making a start. Leroy (age 7) was working in a group which had decided to write individual stories about space and fancied the notion of 'The day I met a . . .' as a theme for their publication. Tossing ideas around had actually limited Leroy's choices and he was rather worried:

Leroy	I really wanted to write about Star Wars but we didn't talk about that.
Teacher	Well that's OK. We said people could decide.
Leroy	Mm but then I can't put the day I met anything then.
Teacher	You don't have to put that either, do you? What's going to be in the story? You need a title, don't you?
Leroy	I think I'll start – I know I met a UFO – but perhaps that'll be the first line – or the title?
Teacher	What do you think will be better?
Leroy	It'll be the title. Then I can say where in the story.
Teacher	Good idea. Sounds fine . . .

Talking: A tool for learning

A very limited range of the purposes for which talk is used in classrooms has been described. The examples were all drawn from infant classrooms but talking to learn should not be restricted to these. With very young children, their language is idiosyncratic; the result of their particular experience and their interpretations of that experience. Teachers of these children have to use their wider expertise and knowledge about language use to 'de-centre', to see things from the point of view of the child. They sometimes have to make inspired guesses about children's meanings. They know that the ability to talk fluently about something or use a particular word can mask an uncertain grasp of a concept. As an example, a four-year-old recently learned the word 'diplomatic'. She was advised to be diplomatic when deciding whether to eat Granny's cake or Mummy's cake. So she can use the word – but only when we are talking about cake! Young children can discuss the abstract as well as the here and now but only if the context makes sense to them. But the struggle to meet with and understand the other mind through speech is a human characteristic not confined to the infant school. It may be that it is precisely because all our attempts to communicate are less than perfect, that talking is such a powerful tool for learning.

*

TALKING POINTS

Can you think of other examples where children show their understanding of concepts like 'diplomatic'?

Are you able to provide children with a private opportunity to talk with their teacher about other matters?

How can we provide contexts which foster the development of more abstract understanding?

Reading for Real from the Start

Henrietta Dombey

> At the end of the Summer Term all the children in my reception class believe they can read. None of them thinks she is a failure.

So speaks Irene, a teacher in a school serving a depressed housing estate on the edge of a small county town. The elder brothers and sisters of these children certainly had a less confident start than this.

Is this confidence justified? In many ways these children can't yet read: few of them would score above their age-norms on a standardised reading test. But all of them enjoy books and have had many pleasurable experiences making sense of them. They 'read' books with evident pleasure and have plenty of opportunity to do so.

This Autumn Term Irene has the top infants and Alison has the reception class, but this year's reception experience with Alison is very similar to last year's with Irene. Just out of her probationary year, Alison shares Irene's enthusiasm for a real book approach to early reading. I've been working with Alison one day a week, finding out what goes on and sharing in the enjoyable process of initiating children into books. I'd like to describe what has happened at various times over the last year or two, between Irene, Alison, myself and the children in the reception class, before exploring some issues about learning to read.

All three of us love books ourselves. We chuckle over the antics of Suzanne Gretz's bears and savour the drama of Rosie's perilous walk around the farm. Our over-riding aim is to communicate this enthusiasm and to help children enter the world of story. Reading is presented chiefly as a means to this end. Like the vast majority of reception teachers, Irene and Alison read to the children regularly. But unlike most infant teachers, they don't separate the business of learning to read from this book sharing. The children's initiation into reading and their sense of what reading is, grow out of such shared story-making rather than word tins, phonic games or steady progression through a reading

36

scheme.

Many of the stories we read to them become much loved by the children. Re-readings are demanded and they join in, predicting events or even quoting the text verbatim, thus gaining a valuable command of the patterns and rhythms of written language.

A current favourite in this second half of the Autumn Term, much in demand despite the presence of mailboxes, trash and other strange Americanisms, is a book I brought in a few weeks ago, *Noisy Norah* by Rosemary Wells. Norah, the overlooked middle child, makes her presence felt in an increasingly wild variety of ways. Although the children's interest is sustained, participation ebbs and flows through the story, rising regularly with the repeated chord-striking line 'But Norah had to wait.' The peak of enthusiasm comes at the end with the words ' "But I'm back again!" said Norah with a monumental crash.' Through repeated readings the children are learning to make this story their own. They experience profound satisfaction in the crystallisation of so many of their own feelings of frustration at their attempts to impose their concerns on the people around them, who are probably as constantly pre-occupied with other business as Norah's parents. They also experience huge pleasure in taking possession of the words. At each re-reading they join in more extensively and more exuberantly. Besides this pleasure in story and language, they are also learning about the conventions of the English writing system. With some justification Christopher pointed out last week that this book is confusing because (like so many Picture Lions) the back has the same picture and writing on it as the front. But he still knows which is which, where the story starts and which way the print goes.

We also read 'Big Books', giant format books, with text that can be clearly seen from a distance. As we read these we point to the words, and as the text becomes familiar, the children join in if they want to, as they do with *Noisy Norah*, or even take over parts of the story for themselves.

As well as producing the words of the story, they are learning to match the words in their heads with those on the page as they chant.

> In went the cow, wishy-washy, wishy-washy,
> In went the pig, wishy-washy, wishy-washy.

The business of learning to recognise words in print has not been removed from the context that gives it its sense of purpose – enjoying a story. The voluntary nature of the joining in removes the pressure of performance, but it's the familiar story context that makes this 'reading' purposeful and possible. It provides a sense of satisfaction in the creation of a satisfying meaning and also the context clues that we all rely on when we are identifying words in a running text. The children may get some of the words wrong, but their contributions make sense in the context. They may read 'said' as 'cried', but they don't ever read it as 'sad'.

Every week Alison and the children make a Class Book, an account of something they have done, or a story created together. One of their favourites at the moment is a book made with the ten full-time children, called *Funny Things Can Happen on the Way to School*, in which, with the aid of Alison's narration, each of the ten children tells of a fantastic encounter, such as 'Tanya saw Postman Pat' while a sceptical worm asks from the corner of the page, ' "Did she really?" ' These Class Books are read in the same way as the Big Books, and give a particular pleasure and sense of ownership of the written word.

The children also do a lot of 'reading' on their own. During free play activities there are always one or two in the book corner where *Noisy Norah* and *Funny Things Can Happen* are among the books pored over, talked about and read. If they can't remember or otherwise identify the words, they talk their way through the books, guided by the pictures, by their overall memory of the story, by what they know of how stories work and by their experience of the language of stories.

As the year progresses, these unsupervised encounters with books are formalised. By the summer the children have a quiet reading time for ten minutes or so each day, when each child chooses two or three books and sits at a table, quietly turning the pages, perhaps talking her way through the story or even making a close approximation to the printed text. Every child appears to enjoy this activity. Some of their books come from the Story Chest reading scheme, but the vast majority are real books, written for children to enjoy.

Most Infant teachers spend a large proportion of their time listening to children read. Irene and Alison see their role rather differently. Their aim is not to hear each child read a page or two every day, but to work towards sharing a whole book with each child at least three times a week, by the end of the summer term. The child always chooses the book, and the teacher takes the role of supportive adult, who tolerates false starts, self-corrections and pauses for thought, even miscues where they make acceptable sense. She also supplies words that the child can't identify, or initial sounds if she thinks these might edge the child towards the words on the page. Most importantly she helps the child make the story mean something personal. This may involve her in doing most, if not all, of the reading, particularly in the early stages or if the book is more challenging than usual.

Certainly she always tries to ensure that this shared book reading is a pleasurable and enriching experience for the child. The extract that follows comes from a transcript of Irene sharing a book with Ian, with others gathered round to enjoy the story too. Though it lacks the stress, pauses and intonation patterns of the tape itself, it shows something of the complexity and subtlety of this supportive role. The underlining indicates the words being read and the curly brackets show where two people are talking simultaneously.

	Spoken Words	Printed text
Teacher	Let's see, what's this one called?	
Ian	How do you put it on?	How do I put it on?
Teacher	How do I put it { on?	Shigeo Watanabe
Ian	{ on.	Illust. by Yasuo Ohtomo
		(*Picture of naked, wondering bear*)
Teacher	Oho, let's see	
Lee	He's a stupid boy	
Teacher	Is he?	
Ian	{ Yes	
Teacher	{ (*laughter*)	
Teacher	This	This is my shirt
Ian	is { my shirt	(*Picture of shirt*)
Teacher	{ my shirt	
Ian	{ Do I put it on like this?	Do I put it on like this?
Lee	{ (*laughter*)	(*Picture of bear wearing shirt as trousers*)
Teacher	Does he put it on like this?	
Ian	No! {	No!
Lee	{ No!	

Teacher	No! (*laughter*)	
Ian	I put it { on,	I put my shirt over
Teacher	{ my,	my head
	shirt o { ver	(*Picture of bear wearing*
Ian	shirt } er my head.	*shirt conventionally*)
Teacher	Huh, that's better!	
Ian	Do,	These are my pants
Teacher	These	(*Picture of pants*)
Ian	are my pants.	
Ian	Do I put them on like this?	Do I put them on like this?
Teacher	Huhu!	(*Picture of bear putting*
		pants over his head)
	Does he put them on like that?	
Ian	Let's see! (*turns page*)	
	No!	No!
Teacher	(*laughter*) { (No!	
Ian	{ (*laughter*)	
	I put { my	I put my legs through
Teacher	{ my legs through	my pants
	my pants.	(*Picture of bear wearing*
Ian	pants.	*pants conventionally*)

When Ian is unsure of a word, Irene reads it, without waiting for him to lose the thread. Sometimes she corrects a miscue where it interferes with the sense. But she withdraws whenever she feels Ian can cope. Irene intersperses the reading with comments, such as 'Huh, that's better!' But these are about the story, not about how well Ian is doing. The reading is not a performative ordeal but, as their laughter shows, the occasion for shared enjoyment of a printed text. Ian's reading is a means to an enjoyable end, or even perhaps, an enjoyable end in itself.

Ian doesn't read only in school. Every day, like all the others, he takes a book home to share with a parent or sibling. All the mothers (and some fathers) of the reception children have been prepared to help their children by a formal talk and plenty of informal chats. Most find it refreshingly enjoyable and eagerly fill in the record sheet that goes home with the books.

Even parents who lack confidence in their own ability to read seem to enjoy helping their children make sense of the stories they take home. One such mother came into school one morning recently with quite a challenging fairy story that her daughter had taken home the night before. Pointing to the word 'gnome' she said:

We couldn't get that one at first, but we puzzled it out and knew it had to be 'goblin'.

However, in this reception classroom reading isn't confined to stories. There are labels on storage boxes, a board for messages and memos and a daily menu. These are there for a purpose: each label or notice gives information that will help the children and their teacher go through the day successfully, and so they are read.

Many of the children notice features of words and letters, and talk about these with evident interest.

' "catch", that's got "cat" in it'

'That one says my name!'

They don't have any planned phonics teaching, but this certainly doesn't mean they are learning nothing about how our alphabetic writing system works. However, the lesson that is learnt most deeply by all the children is that reading is useful, enjoyable and possible.

Irene and Alison don't want to go back to a reading scheme. But perhaps we should think carefully about what these children are gaining and whether there is anything important that they might be losing from an approach that looks like the abandonment of the conventional wisdom of decades, if not centuries.

Learning to read doesn't start when a child enters the reception class. We live in a print-saturated society and three-year-olds have begun to find their way around in it. They can tell a story book from a cookery book, know that the writing on the coffee jar tells you what's inside and have no difficulty in picking out the sign that says MacDonald's.

So pre-school children know something of what reading is for, and have some experience of putting this knowledge to use. Some may also have been read to extensively at home and thus have experience of making stories of their own, of sharing Max's rejection in *Where the Wild Things Are*, savouring the idiosyncracies of *Ant and Bee* or living the threat of Mr McGregor in *Peter Rabbit*. For them the printed word is more than a useful informative device: it is already a means of making sense of the world and their place in it and of enjoying the process of doing so.

Children come to school with several years' experience of word and sentence structures and of the meanings that these linguistic forms can embody. This is relevant knowledge which, if they are allowed to guess, can assist them substantially in the business of word identification. Those who have been read to extensively have the added advantage of familiarity with the distinctive forms and meanings of written language, and so their guesses are likely to be particularly apt.

When they arrive in the reception class, all children (except those who can already do so) bring an expectation that this is where they will learn to read, to make sense of unfamiliar texts without adult help. Our job is to ensure that they can move towards wider experiences of reading and greater independence. To concentrate on the technicalities of decoding, whether by flashcards or phonic games, is to remove reading from the business of making sense of the world and to turn it into the production of a set of empty mechanical responses to the teacher's demands.

As Ken Goodman has said, the teaching of reading has suffered in this century from being technologised. If we look at the success story, the learning of oral language in the home, we can see from the vast array of studies over the last twenty years that it is a rich, complex, and above all purposeful activity. It is shaped by the child learners' intentions and interests as they talk with people who care about them, on matters of mutual concern. But the reading technologists, in their attempts to make the business of learning to read easier, actually made it harder. Guided by simplistic behaviouristic notions of what reading and learning are about, they dismembered the process of learning to read into discrete elements. They then re-assembled these elements into spuriously logical sequences, added 'attractive' pictures and presented them to children and teachers as 'structured' reading schemes. Always allotted the responding role, never initiating anything themselves, children had to learn to recognise little bits before assembling these into bigger bits. The reading book came only after they'd learnt to recognise the words in the word tins. And when it did come, it was likely to make as much sense read from the back to the front as it did from the front to the back. Of course this is still true of the reading schemes in countless classrooms, particularly of those encountered early on. Just try reading *Ben and Lad* (Ginn 360).

If as parents we tried to teach our children to speak as for decades we've been urged to teach them to read, if we waited until they could master all the sound elements of English before saying any words to them, and then held off until they'd acquired a sizable vocabulary before allowing them to join in the conversation, we'd have armies of silent children arriving in our reception classes.

Shaping intentions and expectations guide the word recognition involved in the reading we all do as experienced adult readers. Certainly we don't rely totally on the graphic information on the page. And anyway, to make sense of this we draw on a vast, complex, but largely tacit knowledge of sound/symbol correspondences and other spelling patterns that we have built up through the experience of purposeful reading. Frank Smith has shown us how the information we have in our heads (about language patterns and also the subject matter of what we're reading) complements the graphic information on the page, which calls for our knowledge of sound/symbol relations and other spelling patterns. The more we know about the subject matter of the text we are reading, the fuzzier the print we can cope with.

Children bring with them into school a wide experience of life and language. They have plenty of relevant information in the head. Not as much as you and I have, but plenty to be going on with. Most of them, however, can make little use of the graphic information on the page. If they are to learn to do so purposefully, with confidence and in harmony with the information in the head, they need to be allowed to do what they can already do well. They need to be allowed to guess. But to do this they need texts that will make them want to guess and texts that use memorable, unstilted language to aid that guessing. Margaret Meek has shown us that where learning to read is experienced as a literary enterprise, the process provides its own rich rewards.

Many of us learnt to read in spite of the instructions we were given in our reading lessons in the infant school. We didn't 'sound out' every word not immediately recognised, and we didn't confine our attempts to read to *Janet and John* or *The Beacon Readers*. And some of us were taught by teachers who trusted their own intuitions and taught many unscheduled (and even unconscious) lessons about reading. One or two of us may even have learnt to read without being marched through the numbered books up the numbered levels in relentless, unremitting progress. For there have always been a few teachers who have rejected the arid world of the reading scheme and the laborious time-consuming business of phonics teaching, having found that given good books, freedom of choice and plenty of adult support, children can learn to read no less successfully than their marshalled age-mates, even as measured by reading tests. I threw out *Janet and John* in the early sixties, preferring to offer my non-reading seven-year-olds *Dr Seuss* and *Little Bear*. The children made considerable progress, even as measured on that inadequate instrument, the *Schonell Graded Word Reading Test.*

But what is impelling increasing numbers of teachers to resist the blandishments of the reading scheme publishers and choose instead to offer their children the chance to 'read for real' from the start, is the awareness that whereas real books can teach every positive lesson that the reading scheme has to offer, they can also teach many other vital lessons that can be learnt in no other way. Only through real books can children learn how to love books, how to choose books (no easy matter), what it is to have a favourite author, and how through books to extend their experience of life and language. To postpone these lessons until the reading scheme has been traversed to the end (and they go on and on these days, right to the top of Junior School) is to run the very grave risk of communicating the idea that reading is something you do for someone else, or even of putting children off reading for ever as many studies of unsuccessful adult readers testify. Quoting evidence from students involved in an adult literacy scheme, the Bullock Report states:

> Only one common factor emerges: they did not learn from the process of learning to read that it was something other people did for *pleasure*. (HMSO 1975 para 9.11)

Twenty years ago when George, a black seven-and-a-half-year-old, was in the process of moving within a school year from being a non-reader in almost any sense to being a reader who read Ian Serraillier's *The Silver Sword* with total absorption (if some puzzlement) I asked him how come he never learnt to read in the Infants. His reply summed it all up for me. 'What Miss, with them books downstairs? You're joking!' His self-respect would not allow him to submit to the texts or to the circumscribed role that went with them.

In the early stages of learning to read, children need to feel excited by the power of the texts in front of them, supported by adults who want to share this excitement and unpressured by demands for accuracy at the expense of meaning. Now that writers such as Goodman, Smith and Meek have helped us understand what reading is and what learning to read can be about, and now that others such as Moon and Waterland and the NATE Primary Committee (as it used to be called) have shown us the way in practical terms, a rapidly increasing number of Infant teachers have rejected the traditional skill and drill reading scheme approach and are, like Irene, Alison and me, experiencing the pleasure of giving their pupils an introduction to reading that confers a sense of power on the apprentice readers and gives them a flavour of the delights that lie ahead.

*

TALKING POINTS

The following questions might help you review your school's practice in developing reading in the broader sense outlined in this article:

How often is reading the occasion for shared enjoyment in your school?

How much daily experience of 'reading for real' does your school provide for each child?

How many 'real books' are there per child?

How do you record children's progress as developing readers? In particular, does your recording system take account of children's **attitudes** *and* **experience** *as readers as well as of their* **strategies and tactics***?*

. . . into Contexts of Literacy

The classrooms we were taken to in the last two articles showed us talking, learning and reading arising out of *contexts*, the hurly-burly of life in bustling infant classrooms. They were largely 'mainstream' classrooms, where children's first language was English. Our next two writers both work in multicultural infants' schools in London.

Significantly, they both show how children's classroom talk, reading and writing draw upon the diversity of their contexts. Sandra Smidt and her colleagues see cultural diversity as a resource, not a 'problem'. Anginette can write about her Mum's homeland (from memories of stories she's been told?) and about her developing thoughts on war. Two boys whose first language is Gujarati make their first books out of their experiences in Hackney, or out of their imaginings of witches and magic. Again, they draw powerfully upon stories they have heard.

So, in this classroom, literacy is never presented as a value-free technology; it is a rich fabric woven out of children's lives, their experiences, hopes, feelings and imaginings. Sandra Smidt gives herself the time to look at this happening, and reflect upon their learning.

The children of the second writer, Gillian Lathey, have a rich cultural life made up of 'powerful fantasy worlds'. As teachers we often know little of these. Her sensitive unfolding of her children's stories shows how *The A Team*, *Optimus Prime* and *Godzilla* are a part of the lore and language in which the children are immersed. Like Sandra Smidt, she takes seriously the cultural life of her pupils, claiming that the popular fictions her children live by are potential enablers of their development as writers.

The wind blew as to Colombia: Bilingual Readers and Writers.

Sandra Smidt

I start with some observations made on one day during a two year period when I was involved in team-teaching a class in an inner city, multi-lingual school. It is a school that has long had a tradition of genuinely valuing the languages and cultures the children bring to school; that teaches children to read by reading; and that is concerned that the images children encounter in print and pictures are positive. Many of the children are bilingual and, as it is an ILEA school, it is fortunate in being able to choose to spend some of its annual funding on additional staff. For the past several years additional staff have been appointed from the local community and speak our community languages.

It is Wednesday morning. Wednesday is the only day of the week when all three adults are in the class all day. Eva and I team teach and share the administrative load of the school; Willyanna is a Nursery Assistant who teaches with us as part of our team. There are 26 children in the class whose ages range from 4 + to 7. We have, in addition, the support of Liz who works with small groups of children for whom English is a second language and Mehtap who works with the Turkish children.

Anginette is writing. Her mum comes from Colombia and she is very proud of being able to speak Spanish and English equally well. She often sings songs in Spanish and was delighted when I started going to Spanish classes. She took great glee in correcting me, improving my accent, telling me words. We have some books in school (mainly American publications) which are in English and Spanish and Anginette often chooses to take these home to share with her mum. She is just 6.

Earlier a group of children listened to the story of *The Butter Battle Book* (a 'Dr Seuss' book) and some children are writing their ideas about war. I have asked them to try and write words on their own. Anginette has a few words that she can write and she is tackling the task with great enthusiasm. She writes

War is dagrras
and people di. sagrrs
ro nastd and dams
ciil war is wan
the arame camh to faiit.

She reads it back to me very fluently and I then write it for her in a form that other people can read.

War is dangerous and people die.
Soldiers are nasty and bombs kill.
War is when the army comes to fight.

I have learned quite a lot about what Anginette knows about print from her writing. For example, she knows words she often uses like 'is', 'the' and words that are important to her like 'people'. She shows some knowledge of phonics, which we don't teach formally at all at this stage, as evidenced by words like 'ciil' and 'faiit'. She also uses combinations of sounds and the names of letters like 'nast D'. I know that Spanish is relatively easy to decode because the phonic rules appear to be more consistent than English. But does it mean that, for Anginette, the words 'dangerous' and 'soldiers' have the same construction? She takes her work off to show to another teacher. I am amazed to learn from him later that she read to him from my corrected text and not at all fluently.

Sonay and Filiz are listening to a tape recorded story using headphones. I can see that the book is *Titch* and I go over to see what language they are listening to. They are both Turkish speakers, very proud of speaking Turkish and extremely knowledgeable about their language, culture and customs. Recently the school was involved in defending the rights of two of our children threatened with deportation to Turkey. That involvement raised our standing with the Turkish community. The Turkish parents organised a party for all parents, children and staff. They prepared food and had a band and it was the best social event I can remember at the school. The Turkish teacher, Mehtap, works alongside class teachers and encourages children to read and write in Turkish, teaches them songs and dances and reads them stories. Turkish is not only our largest second language group; it has become a 'high status' language in our school.

Sonay and Filiz are fortunate, as are all the other Turkish speakers in the school, because we have on the staff two ancillary workers who speak Turkish. This means that when children first come to school they are able, immediately, to communicate with somebody. The medium of instruction is English, but Turkish children are not made to feel isolated because they are unable to communicate. In a small way we mimic the immersion schools of Canada. Both Filiz and Sonay are able to read and write in both English and Turkish. They often take home books and tapes to share with their families.

Suddenly there is a commotion in the corner. Minh Duc has broken someone's Lego model. He is 5 and has been in school only one term, a recent arrival from Vietnam. He came to school with no English and no-one in the school or known to us in the community speaks Vietnamese. At first he sat on the fringes of groups – looking, listening, and speaking Vietnamese. He liked to copy things into his books and made neat rows of letters and symbols. Now he talks a little. He knows words like 'shut up' and 'good boy'.

His dad, who speaks a little English, taught him to count up to 10 in English and he likes doing manipulations of numbers up to 10. His face lit up when I brought in a book about kites and he talked excitedly in Vietnamese. We have found a book in English and Vietnamese, but it is less accessible to English tongues than, say, Spanish and I cannot make it intelligible to Minh Duc. We use no reading schemes in school. Children choose their books from a good selection of children's literature and picture books. Just recently Minh Duc has started looking at books and listening to simple repetitive stories. He falls about laughing at books showing pictures of naughty or silly children or animals. He loves the small *Story Chest* books and will hoot with laughter and copy everything I say.

Mohammed and Moosa are working with Liz. Liz works with small groups of children in the classroom alongside the class teachers. Often her group includes fluent speakers of English. The children associate Liz with making books. They make wonderful individual books. Sometimes they use the Jumbo typewriter. Sometimes they take photographs or make pop-up books. Often the books are about the children themselves and about their lives. Often they are fantasies about witches or magic. Some-times the books are just in English; sometimes in English and another language. People on the staff, parents and older siblings will help with translations.

Mohammed and Moosa are cousins and part of an enormous extended family. Gujarati is their home language and both boys were very shy and quiet when they first came to school. The first time Moosa was noisy was when he became intrigued at the magical properties of the magnets he was playing with. Both boys have now learned to read and write. They read quite confidently and choose extremely well, each very sure of what type of story he wants on a particular occasion. They take home books and a card on which we write and invite comments. I know that both boys read at home and, since their parents don't read English, it is the extended family of brothers, sisters and grandparents who have supported and encouraged the younger ones.

Reflections

How much wiser am I at the end of the morning's observations? Well, I have confirmed for myself some things I instinctively believe. Children learn and thrive most when they are confident. They are likely to feel confident if there is little conflict between home and school. This has always meant that middle class children are more likely to succeed because schools share the values of home. Second language learners are often seen as a problem. The fact that children may have no English when they come to school is often taken to mean that they know nothing else. And many schools still operate on the assumption that parents who don't speak English don't help their children at home. But all the evidence shows that all children coming to school are already powerful users of language. If we want these children to continue to be powerful users of language and to be sensitive in their responses to the language of others, we have to find ways of appreciating the considerable skills and knowledge they already have.

It follows that we have to regard bilingualism as an asset and not as a handicap. The most obvious way in which schools can show that bilingualism is valued is by *celebrating* linguistic diversity. In many classes, like the one outlined above, one sees evidence of this in terms of wall displays, range of books and the different voices that children use in their own writing. It is worth remembering that language can be celebrated too by talking about language itself. Language diversity, Miller (1983) says, is not only about different languages, but also about variations within languages (dialects, registers, for example) and different uses of language (narrative, poetry, dialogue).

But how are we going to give our bilingual children equal access to the curriculum? In order to develop effective literacy, bilingual children, like all children, need to be actively involved in both generating meaning from text and in expressing their own ideas and thoughts in writing. Any school instruction which focuses more on form than on meaning is likely to destroy children's intrinsic motivation to read and write for pleasure. It follows that classes that take account of the child's struggle to make sense of the world and that view 'errors' as a window into seeing this process in action, will ultimately benefit all children more than classes which break learning down into sequential units. In our classroom we invited the child to be an active agent in the learning process and so offered the child opportunities to be 'apprentices' in the acquisition of literacy. Bilingual children are alongside their monolingual peers in situations where, sometimes, the teacher models writing and reading in sharing situations, or where the children provide models for each other in collaborative learning groups.

We tried to provide the children with what Krashen (1982) calls 'comprehensible input'. This means that the learner of a second language should have access to as many cues as possible into meaning and context-embedded cues are likely to be most helpful. We use picture books, real situations, story props and other cues and this sort of approach is common in most Infant schools. This type of comprehensible input is never grammatically sequenced consciously and, because it is context-embedded, will always be relevant. Compare the situation of bilingual children like Minh Duc laughing away at a funny picture books with the child in a withdrawal group learning the grammatically sequenced responses

> What is this?
> This is an apple.
> Say with me 'This is an apple'.

We can learn a lot from some of the bilingual and heritage language programmes running in schools in Canada and the USA. Evaluations of these programmes provided evidence that *children whose literacy in their first language is fostered show a transfer of literacy skills per se to the second language.* Sonay and Filiz, who are learning to read and write in Turkish, for example, are not only learning Turkish, but developing a deeper conceptual and linguistic proficiency that is strongly related to the development of English literacy and of general academic skills. So, although the surface aspects – things like pronunciation and vocabulary – of Turkish will differ from those of English, Cummins (1984) maintains that there is an underlying proficiency which is common to all languages. If our bilingual children are to have equal access to educational opportunities, then it is up to teachers and schools to examine their practice and, if necessary, to change.

Valuing a child's language promotes harmony between home and school. Children who are respected for their abilities in another language learn to express themselves and to read in English far more quickly and with more enjoyment than children who are taught English in withdrawal classes, who are regarded as needing 'remedial' help or who are taught English in small stages, removed from making sense of the world. This, of course, has implications for how we teach. Perhaps learning is about being prepared to take chances and make guesses that try to make sense of all that is around. Moosa talked loudly about magnets. Minh Duc laughs at children like himself in books.

Six months on:

Now, six months after the morning I shared with you earlier, I look again at some of the children to see how they are getting on.
Anginette, without help, wrote the following:

> on a Monday morning it was so windy and it blew the hut and all of as and the wind blew as to ColomBIA it was beautiful in ColumBIA and one of as wanted to sleep there for once we didn't know how to get back to LONDON so we had to go by plane it was a long jourey But soon we arrived at LONDON airport and we went Back to school

Anginette has written a story with shape – a proper beginning and ending. She uses book language 'on a Monday morning' and she can spell difficult words like beautiful, arrived, airport. She knows that some words start with capital letters and over-generalises this – for example, ColomBIA and But. 'Journey' is mis-spelled and so is 'us' which she consistently writes as 'as'. Anginette is well on the way to becoming a fluent and proficient writer.

Sonay has moved on to the Junior school and continues to make good progress, although I felt a little disappointed about how static her writing and drawing had become. Filiz can now read fluently and with great expression. She, too, can write quite well in English and is now attending a Turkish school on Saturdays along with many other Turkish speakers.

Mohammed and Moosa are both in the Junior school and, although still quiet and shy, are making steady progress. At an assembly recently I heard Mohammed read a piece he had written about Carnival and was amazed at his ability to stand up and read, loudly, his own work in front of so many other children.

Minh Duc moved away from the school and we have lost all trace of him.

They are, each of them, enjoying reading and writing, taking risks and growing in confidence. The practice in the classroom which has led them to this has not been *different* from that described by Deirdre Pettitt or by Henrietta Dombey in their,

53

largely monolingual, classrooms. Moreover, the diversity and the bilingualism has been celebrated. I leave you to guess at the experience of movement, journey, transition and change that has given rise to Anginette's story . . . But she has *used* them as powerful enablers in her writing. I learn, from my looking, that the diversity is a resource.

*

TALKING POINTS

Thinking of 'diversity as a resource', how do you use this resource in your classroom?

How many books and pictures reflect the mutli-cultural, multi-racial and multi-lingual nature of society?

For areas like Wales and Cornwall there are materials in the appropriate Celtic language. How else could you reflect the language resources of the local area where you work?

ACTIVITIES

Children, whether bilingual or monolingual, often have certain usages special to them. Anne, the girl in Linnea Timson's article on writing (p. 97), was very fond of the word 'weird'. Try to collect some of these usages and share them with the class. Ask the children to contribute favourite phrases and words from home.

What other activities could a school do to help children look more closely at their own use of language?

Taking on the 'Transformers': The Media and Young Children's Fiction

Gillian Lathey

Any writer's work is rooted in his or her own particular cultural background and context. Children write about their families and friends and events in their own lives. Inspiration for fiction may come from their own direct experiences, from stories they have heard or read at home and school, and from the enormously powerful fantasy worlds generated by television series and films, comics and toys. It is all too easy for us as teachers to allow our own distaste for the crudeness and over-emphasis on violence in some programmes and films to prevent us from taking children's culture seriously. We should be careful not to convey the message to children that media-inspired writing is somehow less acceptable than work based on, say, stories we have read to them in school.

There is no doubt that children do love to draw and paint as well as talk and write about the current contenders for a place in their imaginations. I teach in a multi-cultural infants school in London, where the children often share animated recollections of episodes from television programmes or films, and their excitement is infectious. So how do we deal with these powerful influences? I suggest that first of all we keep in touch, since the turnover is fast. In my classroom the *Star Wars* phenomenon has already faded, and the favourites of the moment are the *Superman* films and their spin-offs ('Superted' and 'Supergran' etc.) and the television series *The Transformers*. 'Transformers' are so-called 'autobots' from the planet Cybertron which can disguise themselves as various vehicles and are engaged in a titanic struggle with the evil 'Decepticons'. No doubt another film or T.V. series will have superseded *The Transformers* by the time this article appears.

Initially, of course, children want to draw, paint or model their favourite media characters, and any writing by younger children is often simply a descriptive caption:

This is my mum and my A-team car!

(*The A-team* is a T.V. series about a motley crew of Vietnam veterans battling against wrongdoers.)
Or:

> that is Jazz and Optimus Prime and Megatron and Grimlock

This child clearly loves the sound of the names of the autobots from *The Transformers*.

The drawings and the situations described gradually become more complex. Often figures from different television series and films are featured in the same adventure or are introduced into real-life situations. Shane, aged six, wrote about Superman grazing his face in the playground, surely a rather mundane injury for a being with his powers. Paul, a six-year-old Thai boy whose writing is based almost exclusively on his comic and television inspired fantasy world, describes a visit to the zoo in Bangkok:

> I can go to the zoo and it was hot. We walk far away we saw a lion. The lion ate us up. The lion walked. He-man and Battlecat and Orkel and Hordak fight the Transformers and Optimus Prime and Megatron and the A-team.

An account of a real event enters the realm of fantasy with a devouring lion and concludes with a full-scale battle between heroes from various comics and a combined force of characters from two different television series. Similarly, a description of an outing to Thorpe Park ends in a meeting with Godzilla. Paul is at present so preoccupied with his fantasy world that he writes constantly about the super-heroes which people his imagination and which dominate even his own remembered experience. It remains to be seen how his writing will develop and how this confusion is resolved.

I have also found the media to be one of the greatest sources of inspiration for books which children make themselves, sometimes written over a period of weeks. Those children who are already capable of writing such sustained pieces of fiction do not simply re-tell a remembered film or T.V. plot. Each child features a chosen figure in adventures and situations of his or her own invention. So popular is this writing activity that one Bangladeshi boy took his book home to continue it with his sister's help, while another child – Shaka, aged six – wrote, illustrated and designed a two-volume work entitled 'The Transformers' at home. Shaka uses the mythology of the television series to create his own carefully plotted story about a battle between a 'Transformer' and an 'Evil Decepticon'. This really is a story which includes dialogue and a happy ending.

Sheryl, also six, has written a complete book with delightfully detailed felt-pen illustrations about 'Supermouse'. Supermouse has birthday parties, steals cabbages and ice-cream, gets caught in the rain and travels to Wales – the home of Sheryl's much-loved grandparents. Supermouse does not seem to possess any fantastic powers beyond the ability to fly, and these 'adventures' are anchored in reality and everyday life.

Quite different is the writing of one seven-year-old boy who has great difficulty controlling his own aggression. He started a book about Rocky (hero of the film *Rocky IV*) who 'bopped the Russian on the nose' and 'bashed him like a banana'. After two pages Rocky is forgotten and an extra-terrestrial being called Grogey – no doubt also media inspired – is introduced into the story. Grogey suffers from uncontrollable fits of temper like the author's own:

> Grogey got so mad that he turned yellow. He blew off his steam like a bottle of Coke.

In another attack of fury Grogey turns black and green:

> He got so mad that Grogey blew up his toes and they bounced off like baked beans.

This is written by a boy who has in fact tried to injure himself. The imagery is funny, and at the same time vivid and powerful, reflecting the emotional content of the writing.

Another child already has a well-developed narrative style in his book, the result of many hours spent at home listening to *Storyteller* tapes. His story about an iron spider seen on television the night before begins:

> The iron spider spins evil webs and it is very big. Nearby there lived a kingdom and in that kingdom there lived a knight. The knight saw the spider . . .

This glimpse of a wide range of style and content in young children's fiction inspired by the media reveals the depth and scope of their imaginary worlds. We now live in the video as well as the film and television age and any attempt at direct resistance to the media's influence is futile. The *Transformers* series has already spawned books and tapes, toys, watches which transform into robots, comics and stickers – and marketing is aggressive. Of course this does not mean that we should immerse ourselves in children's culture to the point of suspending all criticism. The boy who wrote about Rocky had already seen the film *Rocky IV*. Only by accepting his reactions in the form of writing and pictures would it ultimately be possible to talk with him about the film's dubious ideology. I have found that in a context where their culture is accepted and discussed, children will eventually reach a stage in their writing where they take control of media figures, placing them in settings of their own creation and writing fiction for their own purposes and in their own style.

*

ACTIVITIES

Ask the children in your class about the books and comics that they have at home.

What are their favourite T.V. programmes, videos, toys and films? Look at these and discuss some examples.

Explore with the children the attitudes and kinds of narrative represented in their reading, viewing and playing outside school.

. . . into Books

It is only in recent years that the *content* of what children read has been on the agenda for the discussion of children acquiring literacy. For too long, we saw reading as a neutral process, something children learned to do in order to get to the real books. Henrietta Dombey reminded us of the power of good texts in teaching readers. Linnea Timson pursues this point, drawing upon her own work in classrooms to reassert the value of literature, suggesting that a school 'policy' should incorporate children's own writing and the provision of time and space for their own talk and discussion.

Shirley Paice turns our attention to the often neglected area of information books, again using her work in the classroom to illuminate ways in which books may be used intelligently and purposefully.

'A Living Through':
Literature in the Classroom

Linnea Timson

Literature: asserting the value

Wind
The invisible Wind
Swaying from side to side
Running to get free!

Angela Critch (9)

Connection
Red as a crayon
Bright as a pen
A nose as nice as the red
evening Sun.

Natasha Bartlett (8)

These two poems of somewhat idiosyncratic syllable pattern, show how two children have created images which add to their, and our, view of the world.

This extension of one's understanding and view of the world is surely what literature is about. Yet the preoccupations with 'language' and 'language development' which were rightly so important following the Bullock Report have perhaps led to an undervaluing of literature in school, leading to literature being seen as only those books which might extend reading and language development.

Rosenblatt (1970) believes that 'Literature provides a living through, not simply knowledge about' and Graves (1983) goes as far as to suggest that children's literature covers 'virtually the entire span of human experience'. If this is so, what are the ways in which we can make it central to the curriculum of the primary school?

To move further, perhaps we need a working definition of what literature is. I see literature as:

> Poetic and fictional reading material which imaginatively engages the reader's attention in an interactive process which s/he considers either enjoyable or useful or both. (Timson 1985)

Within this definition I would include the whole range of poems, stories, novels, descriptions, even comics which could 'imaginatively engage the reader's attention'. Perhaps it is this imaginative engagement which provides a dimension which,

60

while developing reading and language, extends beyond this by contributing to overall personal and emotional development. Readers past and present have testified to the particular role literature has played in their lives. (Grugeon & Walden 1978.) Perhaps we should ask ourselves and our pupils what is the best thing we have ever read, and how we felt about it. The results can be surprising.

Children as Writers

If we see literature in terms of 'a living through' as well as 'know-ledge about' it would seem we should extend this to that literature produced within the school itself. Those stories, poems and descriptions written by the children, and perhaps even by the teacher, can be listened to, talked about and read along with commercially produced material. Donald Graves (1983) describes how this can work in practice. He quotes examples of classrooms which feature an Author of the Week. The author is a child who displays a selection of material, some commercially published and some the child's own 'published' work. It is an interactive display with room for other children to ask questions or add comments.

> Some children list books in order of preference, both with their own writing and the writing of their favorite author. Thus, the child's own writing along with the writing of their favorite author is featured. (Graves 1983)

How this integration of commercially produced literature with the more home grown variety can work in practice is shown by these nine-year-old girls.

> Mary: Sometimes you read a poem or story out of another book and that gives you ideas for one of your own.
>
> Alice: If you write a poem about Summer it might give you an idea about Winter. You might read about something and decide to do the opposite.
>
> Lucy: It might give you ideas if someone's stuck about a verse on Winter. You can look in other people's books and it can give you some ideas.

61

These girls come from a classroom where writing conferences between child and child, and child and teacher are an essential part of the composing process. Lucy's term 'other people's books' therefore refers to both the other children's books and the more 'official' poetry books in the room.

Children as Choosers

Maybe as teachers we do not give sufficient emphasis to the ways in which children can choose their own reading. Fifty years ago A. J. Jenkinson wrote 'Adult tastes are imposed on children, and this is a mistake.' How can we, as adults, make adequate provision for children and how do we involve them more fully in the question of choice and response? Is one way by providing a wide range of material and through allowing children some control?

Work in the field of literary theory (Benton 1978; Hunt 1981) has suggested that quality in literary experience depends on the active participation of the reader. Perhaps it is through allowing children access to innumerable stories and poems, by both established authors and their peers, that we can start this process?

One of Merrill Brown's readers said this about *I am David*:

> This book has great feeling about it. When you read this book you get very involved in it. When something sad happens you feel very sad and when it is glad you feel glad. I thought they ought to have put in a bit more about the children's parents. I think the boy they met should have been more tired, because he was always doing things but he never got tired. I enjoyed this book because it was like a real life story. (Brown, 1976)

Here, this ten-year-old reader, reviewing his choice of book, shows an emotional and intellectual response. He is able to enter into the story to the extent of questioning the author's accuracy and validity, while at the same time demonstrating the power the story had for him.

Elaine Moss (1970) recounts in *The Peppermint Lesson* how a sentimental and badly illustrated book 'was, and still is in a way pure gold' to her daughter and family. Peppermint, a kitten who nobody wants, is given to a child who desperately wants one to take to the school cat show. The kitten is taken home to be beautifully groomed, wins the cat show and lives happily ever after. Alison, the adopted child, related her own experience directly to the story of the rejected kitten, who was discovered and taken lovingly to a home where it was wanted. For as Elaine Moss tell us:

> a book by itself is nothing – a film shown in an empty cinema: one can only assess its value by the light it brings to a child's eye.

Like Elaine Moss, I learnt that lesson from children. I had thought that the Dr Seuss books did not provide an appropriate literary experience for a group of infants. A rather battered set was left around in the classroom and these books were read, talked about and enjoyed for weeks. Whether rightly or wrongly my views about the material were changed through the intervention of the children.

Understanding and Stories

Does not this interaction of children and adults, texts and response, whether sad or happy, encapsulate literary experience? There can be few Primary teachers who would not see story as an essential part of that experience, and Meek (1982) and Wade (1984) provide evidence for the critical role of story in education. Its particular value was explained to me by the pupil who said: 'Sometimes when things are difficult to understand they make up stories about it.'

Stories are valuable as a way of understanding the world in which we live. *Phoebe and the Hot Water Bottles* is a picture story book with a scientific and social message within the story. *Johnny Tremain* is good history as well as a lively adventure story, enabling the reader to come to a better and less chauvinistic understanding of the 'Boston Tea Party'. *The Bonny Pit Laddie* and *The Courage of Andy Robson* by Frederick Grice are not only good stories to read, but an enjoyable way of assimilating some of the geography and history of Northern England. Jane Gardam's *The Hollow Land* is similarly successful both in terms of story and for imparting a feel of the values the Lake District and its people in a way that no text book can do.

Claire's Secret Ambition and *Hannah's Great Decision* by

Charlotte Firmin are picture story books about current social values and the right of a realistic female character to decide about her future life. *Miss Priscilla's Secret*, that of being a teacher *and* a smuggler, led a group I worked with into a long discussion on ethics and the role of the police, customs people and other public servants and helped the children to see a person could be both good and bad. One of the class expressed it this way:

> She's kind of good and bad there. Even though she's a smuggler – she's a good smuggler – bad taking things from people but good giving them to other people.

The role of picture books as an important literary medium is increasingly being recognised. Benton & Fox (1985) explore this, giving the example of Arnold Lobel's *Frog and Toad All Year* where the characters provide an implicit route into the emotions of childhood. 'Toad is beset by the fears, disaster, wonderment and unpredictability of childhood' but 'Frog has the steadiness, knowledge and manner of the resourceful parent.'

It is over ten years since John Cheetham (1976) promoted the idea of using a novel as the basis for a project with specific ideas for achieving this. It could be that picture books like *Not Now Bernard* and *The Tale of Mucky Mabel* which explore the world of children and the distanced insensitivity of the adults could form the centre of a project about childhood and communication – or serve as a basis for children to question ideas about the world in which we live. Many science fiction authors, for example Andre Norton, help children to project into other worlds and to be aware of the need to care for the earth.

This 'Literature across the Curriculum' has a real chance of succeeding in the Primary school. The seven-year-old who insisted on learning Spike Milligan's jingle about the General in the army was learning rather more than an amusing rhyme.

> Said the General of the Army,
> 'I think that war is barmy'
> So he threw away his gun:
> Now he's having much more fun.

This imaginative interactive process has perhaps a particular contribution to make in increasing our understanding of cultures other than our own. As Mercer and Hoyles (1981) point out, many teachers who discovered the Annancy stories through their contact with Afro-Caribbean children 'have since recognized their appeal for young children of all ethnic backgrounds'. Material is increasingly available representing the story and poetic traditions of other cultures. The *Share a Story* material developed in the ILEA and published by Holmes McDougall specifically encourages a shared interaction with stories from different cultures. Poems from different cultures can be found in Morag Styles' collections *I Like That Stuff* and *You'll Love this Stuff* and have been well received by children.

Poetry

While poetry is potentially one of the most life-enhancing activities, it can paradoxically be an area which causes considerable anxiety to the Primary teacher. *Exploring Poetry 5-8* (Balaam and Merrick 1987) and *Literature in the Classroom* (Timson 1985) provide various examples of techniques for getting started.

One London teacher who was very keen on poetry kept books on her desk, read poems to the pupils and helped them to compose collaboratively. Poetry was part of the fabric of the classroom. Incidents were reacted to and exploited, whether it was the window cleaner, building operations or an uninvited wasp. Here is one poem which followed a certain inattention in class.

A Poem on Jokes

In class I tell jokes to Lorna,
She laughs,
Then . . .
          she gets told off.
Then we start again.

Once I told a joke,
About a rubber tree,
She laughed so loud,

The whole class stared,
Then . . .
            We had to write this poem.   (Melanie aged 9)

Practical Ways . . .

Suggestions have been made for increasing the role of the child as writer and reader within the literary framework of the classroom. Are there other ways of increasing the teacher's specific role? Some teachers write stories and poems with and for their children, some teachers are story tellers rather than readers, and still more teachers read their own choice of literature during the time for reading. How else might we demonstrate our particular interest in this area?

One activity which can be tried with children is to let them have a minimum six poems or short literary extracts and ask them, in small groups, to select two to be read aloud to the rest of the class. The choice should be arrived at collaboratively with each group providing reasons for their choice.

Another area which needs to be addressed is the extent to which we have been able to match the family experiences of literature with experiences in the classroom. Is there an ongoing traffic in stories and poems between home and school? Barrie Wade (1984) has demonstrated how a simple leaflet (see pp 67-68) can increase children's experiences of, and ability in, re-telling stories. Although not entirely related to literature, Branston & Provis (1986) have shown how an imaginative partnership programme with parents can lead to greater enjoyment of books by both children and parents. This whole question of partnership between children, parents and teachers is explored in depth in Anne Thomas's article 'Making Connections'. Denny Taylor's work on 'Family Literacy' (1981; 1983) and many teachers' experiences confirm the role of family members, including grandparents and siblings, in children's overall literary and literacy development.

And finally

While thought exists,
Words are alive and literature becomes an escape,
Not from, but into living.   Cyril Connolly
                                                The Unquiet Grave (1945)

66

TELL ME A STORY

Stories are important to your child.

Through stories your child learns more about himself and others. He finds out that reading can be *fun*.

You can help your child by:
1. reading and telling him stories and by
2. letting him tell stories to you.

This guide is to help you to help your child.

ARE YOU SITTING COMFORTABLY?

Choose somewhere quiet where you won't be interrupted.

Sitting side-by-side, or with the child on your lap, will make it easier for you to share the excitement and fun of a printed story. And it's easier to see any pictures!

Choose a time when you're both relaxed. Bedtime for story telling, but any quiet moment during the day can be used.

TALKING AND TELLING STORIES

Encourage your child to talk about the story – e.g. try to guess what's going to happen next.

Let him/her re-tell the story to you in his/her own words.

Ask him/her to tell you stories heard at school.

Talk about your child's day at school.

Use the television – chat about the programmes you have viewed together.

Talk about your shared outings – to the shops, library, relatives, etc.

CHOOSE YOUR TIME

PLEASE Don't interrupt your child's favourite T.V. programme

Don't stop him playing

Don't be over-anxious and criticise

Don't carry on with the story when your child very much wants to be doing something else

With longer stories perhaps:
Stop while he's *still* enjoying the story
Leave him wanting more
Make the reading FUN.

HELP HINTS

It helps your child to realise that writing goes from left to right and that the printed word has meaning if you sometimes follow the words with your finger when reading the story.

If your child shows interest in the print, encourage and help him, BUT don't expect too much too soon. DO let him/her try any words and sentences he/she can recognise. Don't expect this but PRAISE it when it happens.

(Wade 1984)

TALKING POINTS

How do you use the children's own work and choice of material in your classroom?

When do you tell the children your views about a piece of literature?

Where are opportunities created for teachers and pupils to listen to and tell stories and jokes?

'Go and Look It Up Dear':
Information Books in the Classroom

Shirley Paice

'This book seems a bit silly,' remarked a seven-year-old member of my class. 'It says that mother otters have to teach their cubs to swim, and that other book said that they didn't need to learn; they could just get in the water and swim.' That child reading about otters during the course of a class topic was already beginning to look critically at information books. Questioning the validity of a text is a vital part of research, and Neil was taking the first steps in that process. With my help Neil and a small group of interested friends looked at such things as the date of the book, the country which originally published it, and how to find the qualifications of the writer.

Young children accept what we tell them – 'Teacher always knows the answer' – and they readily accept anything printed in a book. Adults are not immune from this: 'It must be true; it was in all the papers.'

Topics and 'topic books'

Many primary schools place great emphasis on topic work. If it involves first-hand experience it can be valuable for children of all ages. I believe that an important part of school topic work is the opportunity it gives us to help children to use information books intelligently and productively. All too often, however, they will use one source book only, copying pictures and even text almost at random. There must be a selection of good, up to date information books available for work on a topic, and children need guidance in working from them.

When the children are young, they will probably be working on a class topic that their teacher has chosen. The resources will have been collected by the teacher from the school and other libraries and presented to the children. This may well be unavoidable, but we should take care to point out that some books are not as reliable as others. There is no harm in including very simple books from series such as Macdonald's Starters and Ladybird Leaders provided everyone is aware of their limitations. Even the youngest children should also see the adult reference books that the teacher is using for his or her own research into the topic.

When working on a topic with my class, I aim to make at least twenty books available to them. The books will range from the simple caption book to adult reference books. I take care to use the latter in the classroom and explain to the children what I am doing. Once I have collected together the reference material I am careful to read it all thoroughly so I can eliminate unsuitable books which are, for example, obviously biased or out of date. With careful research it is often possible also to discover small inaccuracies and inconsistencies, but I do not reject all these books as I find it is valuable for small groups of children to discuss and evaluate them for themselves.

I show them how to 'survey' books to see if they will be useful to them: to look at the titles and lists of contents, to select which parts to read, and to consult indexes. The more fluent readers can scan a page. To help the less able I often write down a single significant word and ask them to hunt for it. Then we read the appropriate passage together and talk about it.

In our classroom we have many books of all kinds. There are lots of story books. There are word books and dictionaries, and several shelves of non-fiction. I encourage my children to browse regularly among them all.

The Conventions of Non-fiction

Systematic teaching of skills associated with non-fiction reading should be an important part of the curriculum. Children are increasingly expected to find out things for themselves, both in the older primary classes and particularly in their secondary education. They need to learn how to locate a book suitable for their particular purposes, how to use a contents page and index, and how to find relevant information without trying to read any book from cover to cover. They even need to find out the distinction between captions and text. Children will gradually become used to assessing a book as a whole, to reflecting on the text and illustrations and to selecting the actual items they are looking for.

It is sometimes surprising to discover that children often do not understand quite basic conventions of non-fiction. I have a book entitled *The Bee*. The front cover shows a mass of bees, and one child asked me, 'Which one?' I always have to explain that *Early Man* means 'early men, women and children', and *The North Sea Fisherman* means 'all North Sea fishermen'.

The earliest stories on their parents' laps help to prepare children for reading fiction, but the type of 'transactional' prose used in non-fiction is quite alien to the young. I like to read information books to my class so that they hear such expressions as 'the spider's eggs are contained in a silk sac' and 'the auditory nerve takes information received by the cochlea to the brain'. Apart from an unusual vocabulary, the actual language is rather different from the spoken word. The uses of diagram and charts also need to be explained.

Topic work should include an introduction to reference works of all kinds, including such diverse material as maps, phone books, time-tables, cookery books and instruction leaflets. Indeed, the children ought to be learning all kinds of access skills involving the retrieval of information, from microfiche cataloguing to computer data files. There is nothing more soul-destroying than the kind of exercise on reference books sometimes met in English workbooks. The trick is to use the books in a natural way when one particularly requires the information. Primary children can plan journeys, make phone calls, and write letters. When the experience is genuine, the study is serious. For example, if children are allowed to telephone real people they will certainly test and improve their skills with words in alphabetical order in the phone book.

How to Choose Books

Classrooms and libraries should be full of a wide selection of information books to help children with directed and self-initiated research. Unfortunately many schools are full of unusable and unused books. These never wear out and teachers are understandably reluctant to throw them away.

The first impression that any book gives is vital. If the outside of a book is dull, and the format unwelcoming, then it does not matter that the writer may have researched his subject thoroughly. Few children will ever read enough to find this out. I try to provide information books that have a lively, logically arranged text and pictures which actually illustrate it. I look for a contents list, an index, and a bibliography. Regrettably, it is still rare for publishers of young children's books to include any information about the writer's qualifications to write on a specific subject (I have my own opinion about this!)

If a book was published more than five years ago I am cautious about it. Obviously many scientific or technical works will quickly date, but there can be problems with geography and history books as well. For example, we still find the stereotyped Eskimo and his igloo, and the condescending attitude towards black people. Nor am I happy with the practice of purchasing for schools a whole series of information books after reading just one or two. Their reliability can be very uneven, as can the standard of writing. The ideal writer is an enthusiast for the subject matter. He or she may find it difficult to simplify the writing to suit children's linguistic development, but genuine commitment shines through unmistakably.

Teachers can get guidance from some book reviews, particularly those in the *School Librarian* and other educational journals, but there is no substitute for our own thorough reading of any books we present to the children we know. A selection of relevant books can often be made available by the County Library Service. Personally I would always prefer to have a book with an 'in-depth' treatment of a subject from an acknowledged expert rather than the type of fact rag-bag which claims to cover such a wide topic as the 'complete story of transport around the world' – in twenty-four pages!

Working with children and non-fiction is very rewarding and full of surprises. When I read the words 'In the early morning the beehive sprang to life' I was greeted with hearty laughter from my literal-minded six-year-olds.

*

TALKING POINTS AND ACTIVITIES

How good is your school's stock of information books?

Critically examine your bookstock, making a note of what subject areas are well covered by good texts at different levels of difficulty.

Where are the gaps? Make a note of the topics in your collection of information books that are not well covered by good texts at simple, intermediate and higher levels of text difficulty.

What access do your children have to these books? If they are mainly in a central library do the children have ready access to this? Do they know their way around it?

How do you support your children's explorations of information books? To what extent are your older pupils able to generate their own questions and set about finding the answers to them?

*How familiar are your children with adult reference texts such as the Telephone Directory, **T.V. Times** and the **A A Book of the Road**?*

. . . into Knowledge and Understanding in Practice

Shirley Paice ended the previous article by reminding us of the dangers of 'trivialising' knowledge in presenting books to children. Carol Fox and Myra Barrs both extend that idea in the next two articles, looking critically at what is supposed to increase a child's knowledge and understanding, but only too easily becomes no more than routinised practices in classrooms.

Carol Fox takes a close look at 'comprehension', linking it to views of reading and her insights into the ways in which children link new knowledge with their 'action' knowledge and common-sense understandings of the world.

Myra Barrs tracks the historical evidence for refuting the view that language exercises are a preparation for actual language use. Too many course books, with their decontextualised language, offer 'false situations' rather than real opportunities to learn about the exciting diversity of language use.

Comprehension:
Meaningful Activity or Passive Exercise?

Carol Fox

Last year an eight-year-old I know showed me her year's written work for 'English'. One exercise book, two-thirds full, contained her own stories and poems. In a notebook were brief reports on all the books she had read during the school year; they showed that she read a lot from a wide range of fiction and non-fiction, and had firm ideas of what, for her, would constitute a good read. In addition there were two exercise books filled with answers to comprehension tests. They covered topics like 'Bicycles', 'Vesuvius', and 'The Tower of London', and they comprised the bulk of her writing for 'English'. A lot of handwriting practice had been accomplished (but wouldn't a personal poetry anthology accomplish this more purposefully?), she had gained some experience of writing in an impersonal mode (though several areas of the curriculum were initiating these modes anyway), and she had put into sentences some words which were new for her (but would these words, plucked from an arbitrary piece of prose, take root in her mind and be permanently useful?). The answers in her book were ticked and crossed appropriately by the teacher, whose practices in language and literacy were otherwise lively, interesting and enjoyable. Even in classrooms where grammar and punctuation exercises have been dropped, comprehension exercises endure with a surprising tenacity. I want to argue here that they are largely a waste of time.

Comprehension exercises are a trivialisation of what reading is. Frank Smith (1978) explains why words are easier to read than letters, sentences easier than words, and whole paragraphs and stories easier than sentences. This is because we process language in a top-down, rather than bottom-up, way. We do not understand what we read by decoding and synthesizing all the elements into a whole; that would be too laborious for efficient reading and therefore a disincentive to read at all. We all know that to understand a story we do not need to be able to define or even recognise every word the story contains. Instead we use our expectations, based on prior experience, of the whole to make sense of its parts. Anybody who has read stories aloud to very young children will know that the story itself, and the expectations it arouses, will carry the child over all sorts of unusual words and strangely constructed sentences. Young children ask for their favourite stories to be repeated again and again, and over a period of time they sort out the meaning of the parts of the story. With favourite stories they are well motivated to do so. A comprehension exercise, in contrast, takes place in a void. The very nature of the exercise, answering questions about the passage, dictates the kind of passage used; the passages are not usually the kind we want to read again and again, nor is their selection predicated on the development of understanding in the long-term. In fact, it is usually a requirement that these exercises should be accomplished in a short period of time.

Sometimes the compilers of course books for juniors use fiction and poetry, and I'll return to these in a moment. More usually the passages are short information texts on random topics. Children are not drawn to the information by their interest in ongoing classroom work; instead their interest is assumed or even irrelevant. At worst the only justification for the passages is that they lend themselves to questioning of a certain kind. One child I know had to do an exercise on a passage called 'Hadrian's Wall'. Though the piece was not linked to any of the current interests of the class this particular child had visited Hadrian's Wall several times and had an excellent first-hand acquaintance with it. However, his own knowledge, his *action* knowledge as Douglas Barnes would call it, had no place in the scheme of the exercise he was called on to perform. What was an exciting part of his real world had temporarily to become unreal and impersonal – Barnes's *school* knowledge (Barnes 1977). What is wrong with this kind of school knowledge is that it promotes, by omitting the child's own experience and curiosity, a passivity which is the opposite of what reading really is – an active engagement with a text on the basis of the meanings which are brought to it by the reader.

But what of fiction and poetry as material for comprehension exercises? In reading a good piece of fiction the facts are often not the most striking part of the reading; the experience of entering the imaginary world of the book or the poem may even be powerful enough to distract us from the facts. In the classroom of the eight-year-old I referred to earlier the teacher read poems, stories and novels with her class all the time, and a whole variety of activities arose from these reading experiences, almost always starting from group and whole-class *talk*. There is no need to supplement this rich diet with comprehension tests; in fact it is quite counter-productive to do so, since these exercises can often be a disincentive to read and to write. Once we concede that complete works of fiction are a better basis for comprehension activities than random informational texts, then we may as well acknowledge that exercises should have no place in our class-rooms since reading for meaning is at the centre of our work anyway.

We now turn to the questions themselves. Typically the focus is on the facts contained, sentence by sentence, throughout the passage. The child's task is to proceed through the passage bit by bit until the facts from 1-10 have been reassembled. The questions usually do not draw the reader's attention to what is inferred, suggested, or evoked by the author's words – indeed the passages are sometimes authorless – and there is no reading between or beyond the lines. Tentativeness sits very uneasily with the answers required, for it is *answers* which are sought. Finding the answers is the purpose of the reading, and reading for pleasure, reading to find out something we really want to know, even reading to develop an emergent critical sense, are all subordinated to this one purpose. If you ask children to make up their own questions on a passage the results are often surprising. My students found that children asked questions which were much less trivial and much more profound than expected. In comprehension exercises however the passage is already questioned on the child's behalf, and what shall or shall not be a source of curiosity, surprise, bafflement, or speculation has already been decided. What really happens in this situation is that the child is left out of her own learning. We must ask, What are the facts for? Only the child knows what information is needed for what purposes in her activities in and out of school. The same is true for 'vocabulary' questions which often appear in comprehension exercises. We learn new words because we need them to think with; they become part of our language if we need and have the chance to use them in a variety of contexts over a period of time which is considerably longer than the half hour or so required for an exercise. Moy and Raleigh (1980) have shown very clearly in their passage 'The Glombots', which uses nonsense words throughout, how it is possible to incorporate words into comprehension answers with no understanding of their meaning at all. The requirement that the reader should answer in her own words leads to further difficulties. Stories and poems are what Suzanne Langer calls 'presentational symbols' (1942), where form and content are so inextricably linked that these forms are not translatable into other forms or words. If we want children to show that they have grasped the concept contained by a word by using other words, then we must ask them to *talk*, and to talk in such a way that they can try things out, take risks, think aloud, be exploratory, use language to learn.

Comprehension exercises test completed knowledge, what the child can accomplish independently. Vygotsky (1978) was very critical of such methods of assessment. He proposed that it would be more profitable and revealing if we looked at the child's *potential* understanding by seeing what she can accomplish with some help from an adult or a peer. He called the gap between completed knowledge and knowlege which can be attained with some help from others the 'zone of proximal development': what we may not be able to do on our own today we may achieve tomorrow in collaboration with others. Perhaps the greatest limitation of comprehension exercises is that they make no room for learning of this kind because they are essentially tests.

Is there no place for close reading with junior school children, no way in which texts can be scrutinized carefully? There are surely many contexts in which careful reading is absolutely essential. Some kinds of fiction demand it, for example fantasy game books. Children who enjoy these games stories find that they must read the rules of the game very carefully indeed and return to them several times if they are ever to enter the stories. Poetry and plays often demand close reading for a variety of purposes, ranging from reading aloud well to the discovery of several layers of meaning. Instructions, arguments, maps, letters and plans all often require more than cursory reading if we are to be able to act upon them. In contrast to these rather practical purposes of reading, stories and poems lead us to make rather different kinds of meaning; we do not act as a result of these meanings so much as experience and savour them. It is the experience offered by imaginative literature which is so difficult to probe through comprehension questions. Talk, in small groups of peers, or with the teacher or a friend, is much more likely to capture the nature of a child's response. Close and careful reading is what most comprehension exercises are not about, since the questions often pre-empt our making sense of the texts in our own ways. We *do* need to know that our pupils are reading with understanding, and that they can use reading for a variety of purposes, but comprehension tests are a closed system referring only to themselves.

We need to elicit from our pupils their own genuine curiosity questions about what they read. We need to encourage them to talk to us and to one another about what *they* want to know. We need to give them time to find their own questions and the time to answer their own questions. Comprehension exercises are curiously devoid of real problems; on the contrary the answers are usually boringly recoverable by the mechanism of repeating what the author has said. We need to develop children's own book and story reviews by making sure that the reviews are genuinely intended to be read by others. We need to help children to read between the lines by inviting them to expand some of the texts they read – 'writing in' a part of the story the author has not made explicit, adding a chapter, predicting alternative endings: there are many creative ways of filling in the gaps in the text which call for real understanding. Comprehension tests call up quiet classrooms, children busy writing with their heads down, yet a classroom where language is being used to learn, to think, to plan, or to discover will above all be a *talkative* place.

*

TALKING POINTS

Discuss how your policies and practices in topic work, Science or Mathematics help your children to make sense of the language they encounter in these areas.

ACTIVITY

What practices can you devise for a particular class or group that would usefully encourage and develop the children's understanding of literary language?

Blanks in Teaching

Myra Barrs

Put the following into the past tense: How (you, learn) your own language? (It, be) by filling in a lot of blanks? (Your parents, drill) you in the use of irregular verb forms in your cot? (You, spend) hours learning the difference between ' a futile exercise' (sing) and 'some futile exercises' (plur)? In short, (you, learn) by performing mechanical operations on artificial language, or by being a language *user*, in real language contexts, from your earliest childhood?

English exercises are back in earnest. What is more, they're back in bulk. Megatons of them are delivered daily, and in publishers' catalogues new versions and editions stretch out to the crack of doom. What is going on? Well it isn't hard to guess. Back to basics is still the fashionable, boring cry. The HMI have pointed out with unusual force that there is definitely no lack of emphasis on basic skills in schools, and that the challenge is now to offer a richer curriculum, one in which reading, writing and mathematics are used for real and interesting purposes. But publishers go on commissioning the same kind of dull, routine, and dammit, *ineffectual* books of drills – and schools go on buying them.

It may be helpful here to glance at the empirical research that has, again and again in this century, demonstrated the ineffectualness of language exercises as a preparation for actual language use. Since the turn of the century, a steady stream of researchers have published papers which have in one way or another, shown that practising grammar points in a vacuum does not improve children's actual written English. A useful summary of this work can be found at the end of the first chapter of Andrew Wilkinson's *The Foundations of Language*. From the list, we may pick out the work of Boraas (1917) who 'found higher correlations between scores in grammar, history and arithmetic than between those in grammar and those in composition'. (This study is similar to a recent piece of independent research by a teacher who found that his class's performance on SRA predicted their performance in mathematics, but not their performance in English.) Then there was Macauley's study in 1947, which suggested that the teaching of grammar might actually hinder rather than help the development of pupils' written English, simply because of the amount of time it required. Heath (1962) showed that a group of pupils who were taught 'library-centred English', with no grammar exercises, were, after nine months, significantly ahead in composition compared with another group who had had a traditional 'classroom-centred' programme of English, including English exercises.

In America, John Mellon (1969) did an exhaustive study of research on the relationship between formal grammar instruction and writing skill. The results of his investigations were unambiguous: he did not find a single study to support the idea that instruction in grammar improves writing. More recently, in New Zealand, a study of the effect of teaching traditional grammar, transformational grammar, or no grammar at all to three groups of secondary school students concluded that 'English grammar, whether traditional or transformational, has virtually no influence on the language growth of typical secondary school students'. Lucy Calkins (1980) found that a class of nine-year-old children who had no formal instruction in punctuation, but who were in a writing classroom where they used punctuation all the time, were able to explain almost three times as many kinds of punctuation as another class of nine-year-olds in the same school who had had much less writing time, but who had studied punctuation systematically through exercises and tests. All this supports the Bullock Committee's belief that 'Explicit instruction out of context is in our view of little value.'

One could go on, but to what purpose? It is all quite clear, for anyone who actually wants to know. An *Horizon* programme showed that teachers of modern languages are making the same point. 'Explicit instruction out of context' – grammar teaching, exercises and drills – is an extraordinarily inefficient way of teaching language. The problem is partly the nature of language itself, which is rule-bound, but often not bound by the kind of normative rules that grammar-book writers seek to impose on it. Partly, however, it is the nature of the human mind that is the stumbling block. Perfectly adapted to the acquisition of language in real human contexts, and to the use of a complex grammar that is inductively and unconsciously acquired, it proves stubbornly intractable to attempts to teach language through deductive methods which require the conscious application of grammatical principles.

These arguments about language acquisition are widely accepted as being true of the spoken language, but not always recognised as being just as relevant to written language development. This, however, is the fundamental point in the case against English exercises. The way to develop as a competent user of the written language is not through practice out of context. It is through writing – and of course, and most importantly, through reading. There are no short cuts. Children who are readers are naturally at an advantage; they are becoming increasingly familiar with the shapes and rhythms of the written language. And children who are writing at length, and who are using written language to express meanings that are important to them, are also learning how to work with the patterns of that language, and make it work for them.

It is astonishing, therefore, that anybody thinks it worthwhile for children to spend time filling in blanks, or putting the apostrophe into the 'brothers-in-law's trousers', when they might actually be using that time for *learning to write*. A look at some of the books of exercises currently in use in British schools, and being published by British publishers at this end of the twentieth century, is a disheartening experience.

The language found in these books is all, of course, artificial language. That is, it has been invented to teach certain language points. Sometimes it is hard to imagine any natural language context in which it might occur. Sententious, pedantic, often surrealistic, it speaks out of an unknown world: 'Terrier, corgi, spaniel and collie are all dogs.' 'Your foot is at the end of your leg.' 'Does that fish come from Brazil?' 'Asking for food, he received nothing but jests and jibes that cut him to the quick.' 'They all, save the smallest boys, volunteered for the boxing contest.' Sometimes whole lines seem to spring out of a Joe Orton play: 'Why did you not deliver Mr. and Mrs. Armitage's *Daily Telegraph*?' 'Cups, saucers and plates were put on the table by Doreen's mother.'

Everybody gets steamed up about the social world of children's books these days; nobody seems to notice that the social world of English exercises is one in which Doreen's mother is always doing the housework, and where social relationships resemble those in prewar novels: 'The hunters met a friendly tribe of

Indians.' 'Father gave his old suit of clothes to a tramp.' 'The general told his men "Do not shoot until you see the whites of their eyes".' 'On top of getting measles, being left out of the team was awful.' 'An archangel is an angel of the highest rank.'

As well as being artificial, over-correct, genteel, always sexist and sometimes racist, the language of English exercises is sanitized. English is, as we know, a language which has no rules, only exceptions. Nobody would every guess, from these ironed-out examples, that using the written language ever presented writers with problems, or that the problems could ever be interesting. There is always one correct way.

When adults are invited to comment on the correctness or incorrectness of, for example, a piece of punctuation, they rarely refer to the 'rules'. They say things like:

'That doesn't sound right.'
'I don't think the second one needs a comma.'
'The rules say that, but it isn't what you'd say.'
'It strikes me as wrong.'

This, in fact, is how most competent writers of English make their decisions about punctuation. They are experienced in the written language, and their sense of its rules is inductively acquired. They have a subtle sense of the use of punctuation for pause and emphasis, and regularly appeal to the ear, to the tune of the language, in coming to a decision. A major objection to English exercises is that they hardly ever appeal to children's actual knowledge of written language. Instead, they teach over-simple rules, and drill them through sentences in which meaning does not matter.

In the absence of a large body of English grammar which is unambiguously right or wrong, the composers of exercise books create their own body of knowledge about language which has nothing to do with grammar and precious little to do with anything else. Children are asked to supply the names for the homes of animals (earths, hives and eyries) or to turn 'masculine' nouns into 'feminine' ones ('The hunter shot the huge tiger'). They 'learn' the abbreviated forms (she'll we'd) that they use every day of their lives with no noticeable difficulty. They learn the singular and the plural forms of ox (oxen) and cannon (cannon). They are drilled in the use of clichés ('Make up sentences which use the following similies: as fresh as a daisy, as pleased as Punch, as dry as dust'). And over and over again they learn about language points that writers of exercise books fear they may get wrong.

With a kind of mad solicitude, the writers of these books continually point out to children the very connexions that they want them to ignore. 'These words are commonly confused' they explain, and proceed to provide children with plenty of practice in confusing them. Off and of; here and hear; their, there and they're; and (the oldest favourite) to, too and two are practised until it is a wonder that there (their, they're) is a child in the land who doesn't confuse them.

But, as everyone knows, when children come to write, however much practice they have had in this kind of decontextualized language use, they make errors. And errors do frighten people. We know much more from linguists now about error and language learning. We know that making errors is a natural part of learning to speak and that errors can often represent imperfectly formulated rules. We know that the same is true of learning a second language and that language learners regularly begin by making certain errors which at a later stage of learning they will correct. We also know that correction has very little effect on error – and that correction is generally too random to be helpful in any case. We know that, as language learners gain more information and more exposure to the language, their language becomes more correct; there is, in Don Holdaway's words, 'a gradual approximation towards correct forms'. But on the whole we are only just beginning to apply these insights to the learning of the written language. The interest in miscue analysis is, however, an indication that, in the case of reading, they have begun to be accepted.

Written errors are possibly more disturbing to us than spoken errors. They are there in black and white, evidence of imperfect learning and also, we fear, imperfect teaching. It is simpler to get the red pen and blot them out than to consider how children can be helped to develop a reader's eye for their own mistakes.

Anxiety about language, in our class-bound society, is never far away. And, as Randolph Quirk points out in *The Use of English*, anxiety about language is particularly marked in the nervous middle classes, who expend a disproportionate amount of energy on a 'shabby obsession with variant forms of English'. So exercises that suggest that you can be one up if you recognize certain uses as unambiguously right or wrong may be popular for that reason. Or, as a book in front of me puts it: 'Different from . . . RIGHT. Different to . . . WRONG. Different than . . . VERY WRONG.' (*The Oxford English Dictionary*, on the other hand, says '*from, to, than*, all used by good writers past and present.')

We can all very easily be made to feel nervous about our own language. And nervousness is a bad basis for taking the kinds of risks that a language user has to take. I am reminded of the boy who said he was making his writing very small 'so they won't see the mistakes.'

It *can* be daunting to see how many errors children make when they write freely. Teachers who do not want to discourage children about their writing are rightly reluctant to point out every error in a young writer's story. Books of exercises *seem* to offer a solution – a place where errors can be marked and right forms practised without so much danger of children being discouraged. Language is split in two, into a part that is 'mechanics' where the 'tools' are sharpened and polished, and a part that is 'creative' where expression, not accuracy, is the thing. Exercises offer a means whereby teachers can believe that they are dealing and, in an accountability climate, be seen to be dealing, with the sharp end of language. But the possibility of such a division is illusory, and the mechanical analogies are inapplicable.

I am not, it seems necessary to stress, arguing against the accurate use of language, or against the study of language as a subject interesting in itself. As a writer and teacher, I naturally find language a subject of absorbing interest, and as an educationalist I want children to have every opportunity to become effective speakers and writers of English. But I am opposed to false solutions, and that is what English exercises are. They reduce the whole fascinating business of the discussion of language to a mechanical exchange, where the child is a filler-in of blanks, and the teacher is a ticker and crosser. Appearing, as they do, in quantity, in the catalogues of *every* educational publisher, they are bought in quantity, and influence practice in very negative ways. And soon, heaven help us all, we shall have Ridout on floppy discs, and the computer screens of the country will be glowing with *to, too, two*. It seems a shame, when all that precious time could be used for learning to **write**.

*　*　*

The following books and courses were referred to:

Haydn Richards: *Junior English*, Ginn; Eileen Sanders: *Primary English*, Blackie; T. G. Ledgard: *Punctuation*, Cassell; Groves & Grimshaw: *Smudge and Chewpen*, Edward Arnold; Fielden Hughes: *Using Commas*, Hart-Davis; Gee & Watson: *The Usborne Book of Better English*, Usborne; Bill Ridgway: *Twelve to Sixteen, A Graded English Course*, Edward Arnold; Sue McCowan: *English Composition*, The Artemis Press; Oliver Gregory: *Oxford Junior English*, Oxford University Press.

*

ACTIVITY

Collect together the comprehension books in use in your school and examine them critically. What important lessons about understanding the written word do they fail to teach?

. . . into Writing

The next two articles both argue for 'purpose and intention' in children's writing. David Thompson claims that we need to build upon the spontaneity and vitality which children show in their talk when helping them to become writers. Linnea Timson demonstrates that if we take seriously *children's* views of themselves as writers, we are helped to see it as a *social* process. Both of the writers, drawing upon their own teaching, emphasise *opportunities* and *audience* as key ideas in thinking about writing.

'Please don't leave the doors open':
Purpose and Intention in Writing

David M. Thompson

> Children want to write. They want to write the first day they attend school. This is no accident. Before they went to school they marked up walls, pavements, newspaper with crayons, chalk, pens or pencils . . . anything that makes a mark. The child's marks say, 'I am'.   (Donald H. Graves 1983)

From my observations of children working in the classroom I can see that they want not only to join the Talkers and Readers Club but also the Writers Club. They are avid writers of lists, jokes, invitations and notes to each other. Personal observations of my three-year-old daughter show me that children 'know about writing' long before they come into school. This piece of her writing was done as part of her natural play; the notation was added by her mother.

They are aware, then, of the conventions and purposes of writing and they use them with excitement and derive great pleasure and satisfaction from this act of communication. Why then do we still find children in our schools who are disenchanted with the writing process?

A writing curriculum which looks no further than the creation of the sentence correct in punctuation, spelling and grammar will not offer a sufficient challenge to the able child or a means of expression to the less able. If this writing curriculum is derived wholly from the teacher or, even worse, from one of a series of course books then it is meaningless to the child. They will be unable to discern any intention or purpose behind the writing. And unless there is intention and purpose then the child might be better not writing.

The ability to talk and converse with others is an important prognosis of the ability to use writing and communicate ideas, messages and so on. Yet, whilst most of the children in our classes talk with considerable skill, many of these children write poorly. They write poorly because they are not being asked to use the knowledge and skills of language, which they use every day in their talking, in any relevant and meaningful way.

Look at these extracts from a conversation between four boys, aged seven and eight, that took place during a lunch break at school. The boys were building a model with junk components garnered from old radios, pumps, motors.

Extract 1

David: This is our engine part isn't it?
Paul: Ian! Ian! We've got a battery at home . . . a big one
Michael: I've got hundreds of batteries . . . big uns.
Graham: No. One of (. . .) car batteries
Michael: I've got one of them.
Paul: I've got a car battery
David: It's got acid in/they leak too much/anyway/anyway (*noise from junk*)
Graham. Come on/now's our chance to get on with (. . .) work/we've got to start from here . . .

Extract 2

> *Michael*:   What(?) about this Dave?
> *Paul*:   Hey! If it's going under water/guess what it needs/screens/
> *Graham*:   I know. What about those . . .
> *Ian*:   (*vehemently*) LIGHTS!
> *Graham*:   You know . . . those sun glass things . . . don't you
> (*background chatter*) . . . that kind of glass/don't we
> *Michael*:   Yea
> *Ian*:   Yea/and I know where to get it
> *Paul*:   (And we need . . .)
>   (*Loud clatter*)
> *Graham*:   Not Mr. T's sun glasses?
> *Ian*:   We can get it from sun glasses.

Extract 3

> *David*:   We are/you can make sparks/you need a lot of buttons to do a lot
> of things
> *Michael*:   Ian! I've just thought/what is i/we'd better have safety things
> . . . what if something goes wrong?
> *Ian*:   Yea
> *Michael*:   I know/Oh no!
> *Paul*:   We'd better have plastic suits on, just in case . . . we have a leak, or
> something.
> *Graham*:   How do we test it out?
> *Paul*:   I know where there's a river.

There is plenty of evidence here of well developed language, of imagination, of humour. Yet these boys had difficulties writing: not so much in the physical act, but in the composition of the sustained prose and of the textbook exercises which was all that had been previously asked of them.

One of the opportunities open to this class for writing was a news/interest board. This is Paul's work after fifteen minutes writing about his sister's accident:

> yesday my sister fel down the stairs. the . . .

And Ian working with Graham on an interview based on a television broadcast wrote:

> Reporter 'when did you notice Eningneg?
> Ozzie when steve and sine

rep. was there a evlop with a ball on?
ozzi yes there was a evlop with a ball on.
rep. Do you now hoor the fiuy strtid?

Finally Michael writing on:

> the fair
> i went to a fair and i went on the roller coaster. i went on
> the ghost-train. and i went on the bumper cars and the
> galloping horses and the aeroplane and the big wheel

Their writing was simple, basic and usually very short. Much of their earlier written work had been derived from text-books. I am sure that what they had been asked to do had been meaningless and irrelevant but is responsible for the difficulties the boys have in writing.

Consider this piece by Matthew (aged 7) writing about water overflowing from a sink:

```
                    a flood
                  run
                    ning
                      down from the top
                        to the floor
        it is                          d
          on                         t  o
           the                       h  o
            stairs                     e   r
                              u n d e r
        and in the bedroom
        t   bed is soaking   w
        h                    e
        e                    t.
```

Matthew is of similar age and ability to the four boys in the transcript and yet he is more at ease with language. He has been asked to use his own language as the basis of his writing throughout his schooling. He has been encouraged to be the main source of ideas rather than use ideas derived from the input of the teacher or from a book. He has worked both on his own and with small groups. He has been encouraged to develop his ideas by talking to his classmates and anyone else he could. He has been encouraged to experiment with letter-shape and letter-size, colour and position in the text in order to best achieve the desired effect. He is aware now that he is as much concerned with the assessment of the developing piece as the teacher and his peers and that this assessment is concerned with the effectiveness of the work within the stated parameters as well as more traditional criteria of spelling, punctuation, length, neatness.

It seems odd to me that when we look to the improvement in reading we look to broaden the base of material to encompass prose and poetry and verse, timetable, notice, recipe and so forth. And yet the emphases in writing often appear to be directed towards the models of descriptive, scientific, technical, historical writing and the various models of the story. All of these are examples of sequential sentence model of writing or prose.

But the writing of the child is not necessarily an end in itself. For the child can be encouraged to see that writing may be a means to an end. Consider Helen's letter to the School, prompted by a request to some children to close doors in order to conserve heat:

to all the teachers and
children

dear teachers and children,
Please don't leave doors open
because it makes us have to
spend the money that we use on books.
If we use oil up by leaving doors open we
cannot buy so much
books for reading and writing and things
like pencils and crayons and things
like that.
Please tell your mums and dads this.
From Helen

Writing is a tool to persuade, instruct, direct, inform and develop meaning and understanding. And it is in the child's environment that the pertinent writing/language models are to be found; models which are using language which is purposeful and pointed, alive, vital and important because it is aimed at the reader's safety, stomach, pocket, needs or deepest desires.

I would suggest that children should be offered the widest range of writing within their capabilities. This is certainly not a new thought but one which is observed more in principle than in practice. If we look at the area of 'imaginative' writing

'Now I want you to write a story that begins "Once upon a time . . ."'

are we offering the child sufficient insight into the structures of the story genre, its varieties, purposes, etc? Are we asking too much of the child when we ask them to write a story within a very limited period? Do we offer sufficient insight into the development of character, of setting, of story development itself? Do we give our children the opportunities to write stories in varying formats: comic-strip, pictures stories, scripts with sound-effects for radio/taping? Do we always ask them to work in isolation? Collaborative story telling can be very productive and amusing when different writers compose the beginning, the middle and the ending. A child can often make positive contributions when working in such a situation which would be unimaginable for her working solo. Consider Jayne. The group she was working with wrote, as a first draft, using M.E.P. Writer,

> WRITER One day Jayne,Clare and James went
> on a treasure hunt.We met at Jaynes house.
> We started just outside the woods . Then we
> turned left to the cottage we went into the
> cottage. in side we met a wood cutter in
> side.we gave him the jam for the key.Then we
> went to the castle and opened the treasure
> chest then Jayne Clare and James went home

Jayne was quite lively and involved when the group redrafted and came up with several suggestions and improvements: 'we went on a treasure hunt because we heard it on the radio' and, about the woodcutter 'He was a nice man with short brown hair'; but when she was working on her own she was withdrawn, nervous of her own abilities. Working with others she appears to cut through her inhibitions and allows herself greater self-esteem.

Returning to the analogy of reading, one of the powerful ideas around is that of USSR-class/school – Uninterrupted, Sustained Silent Reading – when the whole class/school read for a period of time. This includes the teachers, and the head, even the secretary and caretaker. Equally valid would be the teachers writing, performing the tasks we set others and letting our children see us in these tasks, struggling for the right word or phrase, searching for the way ahead and involving them in this problem solving.

What can we ask our children to write? With my classes over the last few years I have tried to make them see their writing as relevant to their work and the life and functions of the school. This has involved them in the creation of posters asking for junk; for parents to help in the class room; for help on outings. They have signposted the school, having decided the positioning of the signs and then the direction to be indicated. They have worked collaboratively to produce radio plays, adverts and jingles. They have composed advertisements for school sales, written letters of invitation and thanks and hand bills extolling the virtues of visiting puppeteers and theatre-groups. And, of course, they have worked on stories and poems.

They have often worked under restrictions of vocabulary, line length, word total when the need to search for a more appropriate, more powerful word becomes apparent. Even the most able children, under these conditions, find that they are challenged.

*

TALKING POINTS

How much 'Please don't leave doors open' writing do you do in your classroom?

Is it possible to show children how their oral ability can help them to develop into competent writers?

What do you see as the most important element in the writing curriculum?

ACTIVITY

Do some writing at your own level next time your class is writing. How many drafts do you need? Can you share your problems with the class?

'We Like To Use Our Own Titles':
Children's Views About Writing

Linnea Timson

Writing is demanding, as indeed we have discovered in producing this book! Many professional writers draft and re-draft. Catherine Cookson re-wrote *Our Kate* eight times until she was satisfied, and Donald Graves made nineteen attempts before arriving at the title of his prize winning essay, 'Balance the Basics: Let Them Write'. So perhaps we need to ask ourselves, how do children, as beginning writers, fare in this process?

Ferreiro and Teberosky have suggested:

> To understand children we must hear their words, follow their explanations, understand their frustrations, and listen to their logic.

However, very often we expect children to hear *our* words, follow *our* explanations and listen to *our* logic. Yet real understanding is likely to depend on the quality of interaction, between child and child and child and adult.

In an attempt to understand this 'quality of interaction', I became involved in an extended discussion with a group of four older Primary pupils. In their classroom, of third and fourth year Juniors, the children are encouraged to write co-operatively, to share their writing, to draft and re-draft their work, with the teacher acting as only one of the readers in the process.

Extract 1

> *L.T.:* When you've written something do you read it to your friends or do you read it to yourself first of all?
> *Anne:* We read it to ourselves first of all and then we give it to a friend – your friends can often pick out points that you don't notice. Sometimes you don't agree with comments made by your friends. Sometimes people have weird ideas.
> *Mary:* If it sounds all right we use it but if it's absolutely weird we don't use it.
> *L.T.:* When you read it to someone else do you choose who you are going to read it to?
> *Mary:* Yes. Well Yes. As long as they give us their stories too.
> *Lucy:* Sometimes you could get even five people to read them.

The above extract gives some of the flavour of the way in which the children's writing is received. I was interested to discover just how far this process went. This second extract shows that while the children did not resolve the question of whether in this process the writing can become more the reader's than the original writer's, it does provide further confirmation of the value of writing as a shared, rather than a solitary, activity.

Extract 2

> *L.T.*: When you read something to someone else and they make suggestions does there come a point when it's more their writing than yours?
> *Lucy and others*: (Very emphatic with laughter) We try not to let that happen!
> *Mary*: It depends . . .
> *Anne*: It depends who the person is
> *Alice*: If you really get stuck you can get someone else to help you and they give you ideas, and they and you put some more of your ideas with it.

These girls very much wanted to use their own ideas and they objected strongly to being told what to write.

Extract 3

> *Anne*: If you can use your imagination I think those are easiest because you write anything . . .
> *Mary*: I'm not very keen about writing set stories.
> *L.T.*: What do you mean by set stories?
> *Mary*: Well if you get a set title and you have to . . .
> *Anne*: Or something there has to be in the story. We like to use our own titles. In the story we're doing to-day we have to have something about Lulu for our radio programme and it's got to be Lulu at school camp. We have to think of something that could be a bit funny but not too hilarious – not too weird and not too stupid – over the top.
> *Lucy*: If you're doing a survey or reports I quite like writing them.
> *Anne*: I'd rather write stories because you can use your imagination so much. In a story you can have people falling down wells. I find stories more exciting.
> *Lucy*: If you've got a survey to do – writing a report – I quite like that because you've got to find out things – that's exciting.

These particular children had followed the initial BBC Domesday Project with a major survey of the village where they live. All the children had been given considerable independence in organizing their work, first discussing as a class, and then in groups, how the survey was to be done. The pupils made their own arrangements to interview residents, distribute question-naires and collate information. This piece of local history work involved a range of activities across the curriculum, and specifi-cally across the language curriculum.

In discussing interviewing the girls make the point that it is necessary to write things down first, and also that when they were interviewing people in the street they needed to write down the replies immediately, but that with arranged interviews in people's homes the tape recorder is used, with the actual writing being done afterwards. Although the terms are not used, these children have seen the necessity for pre-writing activities, the need to obtain an accurate record of what transpires and the value of an *aide memoire* before the interview occurs.

The extract below shows they are fully aware of the interactive nature of the interview and the importance of being well primed with questions.

Extract 4

> *Anne*: If you run out of questions you feel really stupid.
> *L.T.*: Do questions ever occur to you as you're interviewing the person?
> *Several*: Yes. Yes sometimes.
> *Anne*: It depends what you're talking about. If you ask a question and they give you an answer, the answer makes you give them another question.
> *Mary*: If someone asks a question and then the person you're interview-ing answers the question you were going to ask then it's quite hard thinking of questions.
> *Anne*: It's quite exciting planning questions.
> *Lucy*: It's quite hard because you've got to think of things which won't offend people.

The above extract illustrates the idea that talking, listening and the whole social context is related to writing. It is not suggested that all children understand the writing process equally well; the point is that children do in fact understand it much better than is often thought. As Donald Graves has stated, children do want to write, but they need to be provided with both the opportunities and the audiences.

The extract from the *Domesday Anniversary* which follows is not presented as a piece of deathless prose, but as a competent piece of report writing. It is suggested that the provision of an environment where children choose and discuss their work, where their voice is heard and where collaborative work is part of the process, will result in writing being seen as part of learning and much more than just a record of facts and knowledge acquired. This idea is explored at greater length in the National Writing Project Newsletter No 4, Autumn 1986.

Extract from Domesday Anniversary. An example of collaborative effort of pupils with some help from adults and the BBC B Computer.

Questionnaire

Over a 100 people answered the questionnaire and most of the people wanted some new facilities or something different in the village. The most common complaint was about dogs.

People were disgusted with all the stray dogs and all the dogs mess that was around. They wanted more dog control, perhaps even a dog warden! They thought that Pooper Scoopers should be on sale in the local shops and that people should be made to put their dogs on leads at all times. Although the Kerrier District Council have made it illegal for dogs to foul on the footpaths people can't stop the stray dogs as they don't know who their owners are.

Lots of people in Stithians think it is untidy and needs more litter bins. They said that before they put the litter bins up. When they put up litter bins they should put up some signs saying how unhygienic it is not to have them.

Some people thought that Stithians should have a village map with a notice board and details of what is happening in the village, perhaps sited in the front of the school.

Lots of people wanted a Youth Club for the over ten's to help stop vandalism. There is talk of a youth club starting but it is difficult to find a suitable room, because the Church Hall is too busy and a Youth Club would need a permanent place to store their equipment. Many people thought that a proper adventure playground for the under eleven's would be nice as well. A community centre was something many, many people wanted and this might help with some of the other things too.

A lot of people wanted more police and they would like one to live in the village. They thought that a policeman living in the area would stop break-ins and robbery. Parking in Stithians would become more strict, so less children would get knocked over and injured or killed. With a policeman or woman in the village it would be quite quiet without so much unpleasantness.

Many people mostly the old would like a mini bus service. Most people were not at all happy with the bus service that serves the village at the moment, only a couple of people were happy with it. People also said that if they had to put up with it at least they would have to have some new timetables for them to see.

*

Postscript

These girls were followed up a year later (March 1987). They were given a copy of the transcript of their conversation and asked if they still held the same views. They were insistent that they still wanted to choose their own subjects for writing, and that they liked to have their writing read by their peers.

> *Mary*: I don't mind giving my story to other people but I'm not that fussed if I don't get theirs.
> *Anne*: Alice doesn't always give me her stories but I like her to read mine because she gives such good opinions. She's a good opinionist.

These girls had matured to the extent that while the value of another's views was really important to them in the composing process, it was no longer critical if this was not reciprocated. The teacher reported that the girls were enthusiastic, determined and amongst the most creative.

TALKING POINTS

How often do the children in your class have the opportunity to write on a topic of their own choice?

Who reads what the children write?

Who does the writing belong to?

ACTIVITY

Select a group of three to five children whom you think have a variety of competencies as writers and discuss with them what they think about writing and how they see themselves as writers.

Up for Inspection:
One School's Language Policy

The policy which Linda Ashworth offers, and which provided the stimulus for this collection, is not offered as a blueprint, but as a starter for discussion.

1)   What aspects would you incorporate?

2)   What aspects of it would you extend?

3)   Which areas of language and literacy have not been addressed, and which you would wish to develop (e.g., the role of microtechnology)?

A School's Language Policy

Linda Ashworth

INTRODUCTION

Every school has a language policy, whether it is implicit or explicit, consensus or individual, in people's heads or on paper. What I have done is to write about what happens in my school, not what should happen. The notes have been through many stages and drafts. Initially I had discussions with the Head and Deputy, followed by the Infant Team and then the Junior Team. (I am head of the Infant Department.) A language policy is not a static thing. It changes to meet the needs and demands of new staff, new children, a changing society and recent research findings. Nevertheless, I think these notes may be of interest to teachers, advisers and teachers' centres, not as guidelines but rather as a discussion document.

Every school is different and consequently has different needs but most teachers welcome discussion documents because they give a common starting point and often stimulate thought and evaluation and lead to more of a consensus than before the discussions. The starting point for our policy is the children. We look at their interests and needs, both present and future, and organize the ways we 'teach' language around them. Relationships are very important. You get the kind of talk, listening, reading and writing from the child that your relationship and the school environment determines.

A child's language is part of that child. You can't separate them. We value the children and their language. We also see the language arts as interrelated and our language policy takes account of this in relation to the children's needs. For the purpose of this document, however, language has been categorized as follows:

Spoken language: Talking, Listening.
Written language: Reading, Writing.

In each case we considered our aims, strategies, resources and evaluation. Literature has a separate section because of our belief in the importance of story.

There is no separate section for children with special educational needs because we try to treat every child as an individual, not just those with special needs. Everyone has special needs.

Spoken Language A: Talking

Aims

1. To accept, encourage and value children's talk.
2. To encourage children to learn through talk, just as adults do. E.g., If you're trying to solve a problem, talking it through with someone often leads to a solution.
3. To recognize the importance of adults as 'language models' for children to learn from.
4. To recognize the importance of children talking to each other without adults present.

Strategies/Resources

1. We use children's talk as a prime resource for reading and writing. We make their first 'reading books' from their spoken language, using *Breakthrough to Literacy* materials.
2. We give children the time, space and freedom to talk to their friends while they are working. They are encouraged to work with different aged children, brothers and sisters, mums who are helping, the head, caretaker, play-group, etc.
3. Mums, grans, senior citizens, visitors are encouraged to talk to the children and share their experiences. They play reading and maths games with the children – some published games, some made by the children. They share books, cook, sew, knit and help with other craft work.
4. We create opportunities for children to talk in small groups without a teacher present. They play in the play house, invent and play games, improvise plays, often using tapes.
5. Children sometimes make private tapes for their teacher to

listen to. This is something quiet children often do.

6. Children are helped to use technical terms (e.g., those found in published maths schemes) by coming to terms with them in their own words first. E.g., load of, lot of leading to 'set' of.

7. We try to ask open-ended questions to encourage exploratory answers, rather than close-ended questions which often have a one word right or wrong answer.

8. Problem-solving is used as a shared activity in maths or writing. Unsupervised talk is encouraged and children tackle the problem, report back, assess, justify and explain their solution.

9. We create opportunities for children to talk for different functions and audiences. This encourages them to develop different styles appropriate for different situations. E.g., talking to a friend, group of friends, a class, the Infant Dept in Assembly, the whole school in Assembly, showing visitors round, interpreting messages to teachers and children.

10. We try to give children the freedom and time to ask their own questions, make their own judgements and use their own initiative. E.g., when planning their day, discussing with teachers, organizing who they work with and how.

11. We try not to hinder children's language development by our own use of language. We try to keep our styles of talk as informal and as close to the child's as possible whenever appropriate.

Spoken Language B: Listening

Aims

1. To encourage children to listen when others are talking, in order to learn from them.

2. To give children real reasons for listening; active rather than passive listening, leading towards effective communication.

Strategies/Resources

1. Teachers and children put favourite books onto tape for

children to listen to with headphones, and follow the text.

2. Children make tapes about specialist interests for others to listen to. E.g., gold, snooker, stamp-collecting, bird-watching. The tapes are often transcribed and typed into books as a reading resource.

3. Children make tapes reporting events. E.g., holidays, birthday parties, visits. These are often transcribed too, including photographs if possible.

4. Stories are used a great deal. As well as teachers and children telling and reading stories, we use radio, T.V., video, films of stories. E.g., *Words and Pictures* (B.B.C.) *Let's Join In* (Radio), Weston Woods films hired from Schools' Library Service and Rank films for long stories like *Charlotte's Web*.

5. Group and class discussions are encouraged and teachers often sit with children in a circle on the floor. This makes it easier to hear what everyone says. These discussions are sometimes taped and transcribed. A shell or similar object is sometimes used to indicate who is speaking, and to encourage children to take turns and to always listen to the person with the shell. Another way is to ask them to put their finger out when they want to speak. Children sometimes chair the discussions.

6. Children are encouraged to ask real questions of teachers, therefore creating situations where they really listen to the answers. E.g., 'Why are your legs spiky Miss?'

7. Children are encouraged to take an active part in Assemblies, sometimes organizing them, sometimes telling everyone about something of interest to them. Children are often more interested in listening to friends rather than teachers talking about a pet hobby.

8. We try to really listen to children and value what they say. It is important for teachers to show a good listening model, although it takes a lot of self control not to interrupt.

9. We try to take small groups of children out on visits as often as possible instead of class trips once a year. E.g., country walks, city farm, shops, museums, local environment, plant nursery/trout hatchery, bird-watching, etc. There is more opportunity for listening with a small group, although it means that other teachers have a larger number of children during the visit.

10. In discussions we try to give opportunities for reporting and evaluating opinions. Children are encouraged to justify opinions and be prepared to accept and deal with challenges from others.

Written Language A: Reading

So much is said and written about the teaching of reading that we decided to begin by defining our terms of reference. We understand the ability to read to involve making meaning of a text and being critical in evaluating what is read. Fluent reading we understand as doing that independently and usually silently, using a variety of techniques for a range of purposes.

Aims
1. To enable children to read as we've defined it, both from choice for pleasure and to cope effectively with the influence of print in a variety of forms.
2. To foster the reading habit, by demonstrating our enjoyment of reading.

Strategies/Resources

1. We fit the reading to the child, not the child to the reading. We use *Breakthrough to Literacy* materials (Longmans for Schools Council) in the initial stages of literacy, backed up by a wide selection of picture/story books, bought and borrowed from Schools' Library Service. In this way we hope children can find what they want.
2. Children are encouraged to choose what they read from the start and are given as much guidance in this as they need.
3. Very easy books are shelved together as are those with very difficult text but the majority are displayed with covers showing or in book trolleys, without any kind of grading.
4. We try to create a balance between reading for pleasure and more functional reading, both by our resources and by introducing children to formats other than books. E.g., forms, brochures, timetables, labels, notices, etc.
5. As mentioned before, we use children's talk and writing as a

prime reading resource. Their books, typed and 'published' by us, are shelved alongside commercially published ones.

6. We create opportunities for children to read differently for different purposes, in response to their needs. E.g., some older infants made an instruction book for reception children about using tape-recorders.

7. We see pre-reading as an introduction to books and print, not as a series of auditory and visual discrimination activities. We show children how to find their way round books, how to choose, etc.

8. We provide enough flexibility in the timetable to enable children to browse, read at length, take time choosing and read silently without interruption. E.g., everyone silently reads/looks at books at the same time every day, graduating from 5 minutes for reception children to 30 minutes for top infants.

9. Most of the teaching of reading is individual, in reading to teacher time, but some techniques are taught in large groups. E.g., how to find your way round the contents and index of a non-fiction book.

Wherever possible, even in large group situations, we try to respond to the needs and interests of the children. E.g., rather than teaching skimming, scanning and intensive reading techniques by exercises devoid of context, we would show children how to choose a book (skimming), look up words in a dictionary (scanning) and follow instructions (intensive reading).

Written Language B: Writing

Aims

1. To foster the writing habit; to show children the need for writing and the enjoyment it can give when there is a real intention behind it.

2. To teach children about the processes involved in writing, by demonstrating and giving them an adult model. They are encouraged and helped by realizing it's almost as hard for me to compose writing as it is for them.

3. To show them how to write differently for different situations. E.g., a note to a friend, a shopping list, a story for a younger child.

Strategies/Resources

1. We use *Breakthrough to Literacy* materials in the early stages of writing so that children can compose language and learn about its structure without having to physically write the letters and words unless they want to.
2. Much of what we teach is by adult model. E.g., we can introduce letter writing by writing a letter to one of the children, we can write a story for the class, make a menu for the school lunch. This will show them different functions and audiences.
3. We teach letter formation and the physical techniques of writing alongside composition.
4. We create situations in which children's writing produces responses that encourage further writing. E.g., a letter to an author often brings a response which causes the child to write back.
5. We encourage children to write for teachers in ways other than 'for assessment', and we value what they write. E.g., we would often respond to the writing, verbally or in writing, rather than just correcting errors.
6. Children are encouraged to be as independent as possible as early as possible. There are word banks and letter banks as well as dictionaries and children are encouraged to use word-makers (*Breakthrough to Literacy*), as soon as they show an interest in how words are spelled.
7. We encourage children from the early stages to think about writing in draft stages. We don't expect it to be right first time.
8. We create opportunities for 'real' writing as described by Mary Hoffman in *Reading, Writing and Relevance* (Hodder & Stoughton). E.g., school comic or magazine, Christmas cards, letters to Father Christmas, to authors, etc.
9. As with reading most of the teaching of writing is individual, but some techniques are taught in larger groups. E.g., how to make notes.

10. We 'publish' much of the children's writing for themselves and others to read, as suggested by Donald Graves in *Writing: Teachers and Children at Work* Heinemann 1982.
11. Having shown children different kinds of writing, appropriate for different situations, we give them the freedom of choice as to what kind of writing they do. Help is often given individually if children need it, in deciding what kind of writing to do.

Literature

Literature, like reading, often means different things to different people, and so we thought it useful to define it. Any written language which sets out to represent the human condition we would see as literature. That would include novels, stories, T.V. series, and children's writing, but exclude the spoken word and non-fiction.

Aims

1. To give children the opportunity to experience the ideas and feelings of others in order that they can develop a better understanding of themselves and others.
2. To provide a very strong motivation towards reading.

Strategies/Resources

1. As previously mentioned we use children's writing as the first step towards an appreciation of literature.
2. Children are encouraged to read story books as soon as they come to school, instead of graded primers which cannot be defined as literature.
3. We read to children as often as possible and at varying times, not just at the end of the afternoon.
4. We show our own enthusiasms for particular stories and authors, try to know the books that are available and share our responses with the children.
5. From the beginning children have a free choice of what they read.

111

6. We encourage children's responses to literature, both individually and in larger groups. E.g., how did it make you feel? What did you think about Max doing that? etc.
7. Other kinds of responses are encouraged too, although not expected. E.g., reviews, cover designs, letters to authors, posters, own versions of stories, art work, etc.
8. We have a school bookshop (Books for Students, Heathcote Industrial Estate, Warwick) which stocks good, cheap paperbacks for all ages. This encourages children to become book owners.
9. We encourage children to borrow books from school, both our own and library books.
10. We try to be aware of new books and authors by reading reviews in *Child Education*, *School Librarian*, *Signal* book reviews and our own Schools' Library publications. NATE and UKRA are also useful for this purpose.

Evaluation

We encourage children to evaluate what they read and what is read to them. As a staff we have developed criteria for book selection and evaluation: the intrinsic value of the book, aesthetic quality, purpose in writing, interests and needs of the children, bias in terms of race, sex and class and many other factors are all considered. Colleagues' opinions are also important. Children are always consulted about book selection and are taken to Schools' Library Service to help choose those books which are to be borrowed or bought.

Evaluation/Development

As well as evaluating and monitoring children's progress in the language arts we need to evaluate and develop our teaching strategies and resources.

We evaluate and monitor children's progress informally without the use of any 'tests'. We do this by observation, discussion and listening and by recording information which we think will help us to know how to further help the child. We find tapes of children reading or talking and pieces of their writing with commentaries by teachers far more helpful than checklists full of ticks, crosses, stars or whatever. E.g., a child who very rarely spoke would perhaps have a personal tape as part of their profile. Similarly a child who was taking a long time to begin reading would have a tape reading to a teacher and perhaps another reading aloud independently. Physical impediments such as deafness or speech defects would be recorded, plus the action taken.

Most of the assessment of children's progress goes on throughout the day: when they are talking to you or each other, when they are listening to you or their friends, when they are reading to you or independently and when they are writing. We talk to children about their progress, to colleagues, to their parents. We encourage self-assessment both verbal, pictorial and written if they are able to put into writing how they feel about their progress.

When assessing children's reading we are more interested in the strategies they are using than in word accuracy.

When assessing their writing again we are looking for the strategies they are using. Are they able to use sentence-makers/ word-makers independently? Can they use a dictionary? Can they self-correct from one draft to another? Have they moved from personal writing (close to talk) to other modes (story, poem, etc)? Children are encouraged to help with their records by recording books they have read; by selecting pieces of writing to be put into their file which goes throughout the school with them, etc.

We evaluate and develop our resources and teaching strategies by talking to colleagues, informally and in team and staff meetings. We decide jointly on resources and strategies and try to be honest when things don't work out as we'd hoped.

Endword

One Child's View of Reading

John: Course I like reading . . . you see, emm, well, when I was at my old school, I, emm, the first time I used we used to have worls (*indistinct*) and a lot of the time all of my friends got higher than me so you see at the end of that I didn't like it I just didn't like it I just didn't wasn't too interested.

When I got higher up I found I was on a reading scheme that was so boring you see kept on going on and on ploughing through that so I kept on oh . . . (*indistinct*) but really I wanted to read I don't know why it just all came over me that reading might be exciting . . . I heard my Dad talking about something which he read and I thought I might like to have a go at that and my Dad said em well why don't you ask the teacher em if em you could so I asked her and she said no and so I asked her again and she said no and I kept on asking her and in the end she said yes.

So she let me read some of these books and their were too easy and now I've got here there's some better books and *I found you're allowed to read books from home and I just love it and now I've got into the habit of doing it so when I see anything I just read it*

Excerpt from a conversation with John, aged 8, after some months at his new school. Collected by Helena Mitchell, researcher at Brighton Polytechnic.

BIBLIOGRAPHY: Academic Books

BALAAM, Jan and MERRICK, Brian (1987) *Exploring Poetry 5-8.* National Association for the Teaching of English.

BARNES, Douglas (1977) *From Communication to Curriculum* Penguin.

BENTON, M (1978) *The First Two R's. Essays on the process of writing and reading in relation to the teaching of literature* University of Southampton.

BENTON, M & FOX, G (1985) *Teaching Literature. Nine to Fourteen* Oxford University Press.

BRANSTON, P & PROVIS, M (1986) *Children and Parents Enjoying Reading* Hodder & Stoughton.

BROWN, Merrill (1976) 'Reading Together: Eight to Ten Year Olds as Critics' in *Children's Literature in Education 21* Summer 1976.

CALKINS, Lucy (1980) 'Children Learn the Writer's Craft' *Language Arts* 57 pp 107-113.

CHEETHAM, John (1976) 'Quarries in the Primary School' in *Writers, Critics and Children* ed. Fox, G Heinemann Educational Books 1976.

CLARK, Margaret (1976) *Young Fluent Readers* Heinemann Educational Books.

CUMMINS, J (1984) *Bilingualism and Special Education: Issues in Assessment and Pedagogy* Multilingual Matters 6.

DONALDSON, Margaret (1978) *Children's Minds* Fontana.

FERREIRO, Emilia and TEBEROSKY, Ana (1983) *Literacy Before Schooling* Heinemann.

FOX, Carol (1983) 'Talking Like a Book' in *Opening Moves* (ed. Meek, M) Bedford Way Papers no. 17 Institute of Education London

GOODMAN, Kenneth (1982) *Language and Literacy vol. 2* Routledge & Kegan Paul.

GRAVES, Donald H (1976) 'Balance the Basics: Let them Write' (Ford Report) in Graves, D H (1984) *A Researcher Learns To Write* Heinemann.

GRAVES, Donald (1983) *Writing: Teachers and Children at Work* Heinemann Educational Books.

GRIFFITHS, A and HAMILTON, D (1984) *Parent, Teacher, Child: Working Together in Children's Learning* Methuen.

GRUGEON, E & WALDEN, P (1978) *Literature and Learning* Ward Lock Educational in association with the Open University Press.

HMSO (1975) *A Language for Life* Report of the Committee chaired by Sir Alan Bullock.

HMSO (1978) *Primary Education in England* A Survey by H M Inspectors of Schools

HEATH, W G (1962) 'Library-Centred English' *Education Review* 14:2.

HOFFMAN, Mary (1976) *Reading, Writing and Relevance* Hodder & Stoughton.

HOLDAWAY, Don (1979) *The Foundations of Literacy* Ashton Scholastic Sydney.

HOLT, John (1970) *How Children Learn* Penguin.

HUNT, P L (1981) *A Critical Study of English Literature Written for Children* Unpublished Ph.D Thesis, Wales (UWIST).

INGHAM, Jennie (1981) *Books and Reading Development* Heinemann Educational Books.

JENKINSON, A J (1940) *What Do Boys and Girls Read* Methuen.

KRASHEN, S P (1982) *Principles and Practice in Second Language Acquisition* Pergamon.

LANGER, Susanne K (1942) *Philosophy in New Key* Harvard University Press.

MACCAULEY, W J (1947) 'The Difficulty of Grammar' *Brit. J. Ed. Psych.* 17 (November) pp 153–162.

MEEK, Margaret (1982) *Learning to Read* Bodley Head.

MERCER, N & HOYLES, M (1981) *Language in Schools and Community* Edward Arnold.

MILLER, Jane (1983) *Many Voices* Routledge & Kegan Paul.

MOON, Cliff (ed.) (1985) *Practical Ways to Teach Reading* Ward Lock Educational.

MOSS, Elaine (1970) 'The Peppermint Lesson' in *The Cool Web* ed. Meek, M *et al.* (1977) Bodley Head.

MOY, B and RALEIGH, M (1980) 'Comprehension: Bringing it Back Alive' in *The English Magazine* no. 5 ILEA English Centre.

NATE Primary Committee (1984) *Children Reading to Their*

Teachers National Association for the Teaching of English.

National Writing Project (1986) *Newsletter* no. 4 School Curriculum Development Committee.

QUIRK, Randolph (1962) *The Use of English* Longman.

ROSENBLATT, L M (1970) *Literature as Exploration* Heinemann Educational Books.

SMITH, Frank (1978) *Reading* Cambridge University Press.

SMITH, Frank (1974) *Understanding Reading* Holt, Rinehart & Winston.

TAYLOR, D (1981) 'The Family and the Development of Reading Skills' in *Journal of Research in Reading* 4 (2) pp 92–103.

TAYLOR, D (1983) *Family Literacy, Young Children Learning to Read and Write* Heinemann Educational Books.

TIMSON, L G (1985) 'Literature in the Primary School' in *Practical Ways to Teach Reading* ed. Moon, Cliff Ward Lock Educational.

TIZARD, Barbara and HUGHES, Martin (1984) *Young Children Learning* Fontana.

TIZARD, Barbara (1975) *Early Childhood Education* National Foundation for Educational Research.

VYGOTSKY, Lev (1962) *Thought and Language* Massachusetts Institute of Technology Press.

VYGOTSKY, Lev (1978) *Mind in Society* Harvard University Press.

WADE, Barrie (1984) *Story at Home and School* Educational Review. Occasional Publication no. 10 University of Birmingham.

WATERLAND, Liz (1985) *Read With Me: An Apprenticeship Approach to Reading* Thimble Press.

WELLS, Gordon (1981) *Learning Through Interaction* Cambridge University Press.

WELLS, Gordon (1982) *Language, Learning and Education* Centre for the Study of Language and Communication University of Bristol.

WELLS, Gordon (1987) *The Meaning Makers* Hodder & Stoughton.

WIDLAKE, Paul & MacLEOD, Flora (1984) *Raising Standards. Parental Involvement Programmes & Language Performance of Children* CEDC Lyng Hall, Blackberry Lane, Coventry CV2 3JS.

WILKINSON, Andrew M (1971) *The Foundations of Language: Talking and Reading in Young Children* Oxford University Press.

BIBLIOGRAPHY: Children's Books

BANNER, A *Ant and Bee* Kaye & Ward.

FASSETT, J (1922) *Beacon Readers* Ginn.

FIRMIN, Charlotte (1982) *Claire's Secret Ambition* Macmillan.

FIRMIN, Charlotte (1980) *Hannah's Great Decision* Piccolo.

FORBES, Esther (1979) *Johnny Tremain* Puffin.

FURCHGOTT, Terry and DAWSON, Linda (1980) *Phoebe and the Hot Water Bottles* Picture Lions.

GARDAM, Jane (1983) *The Hollow Land* Puffin.

GRETZ, Susan (1981) *Teddy Bears Moving Day* Hippo.

GRICE, Frederick (1980) *Bonny Pit Laddie* Puffin.

GRICE, Frederick (1982) *Courage of Andy Robson* Puffin.

HOLM, Ann (1965) *I am David* Methuen.

HUTCHINS, Pat (1970) *Rosie's Walk* Picture Puffin.
Also available in English and Urdu, English and Greek, and English and Turkish (1987) Bodley Head; and translated into Welsh (1983) Gomer.

HUTCHINS, Pat (1974) *Titch* Picture Puffin.

ILEA *Share a Story* Holmes McDougall.

KEENAN-CHURCH, H (1978) *Ben and Lad* (Reading 360) Ginn.

LOBEL, Arnold (1972) *Frog and Toad All the Year* World's Work Paperbacks.

MCKEE, David (1980) *Not Now Bernard* Andersen Press.

MELSER, J and COWLEY, J (1980) *Mr Wishy Washy* Arnold.

MINARIK, E H (1958) *Little Bear* World's Work.

MURPHY, Jill (1987) *Peace at Last* Macmillan.

O'DONNELL, M and MUNRO, R (1954) *Janet and John* Nisbet.

POTTER, Beatrix (1902) *The Tale of Peter Rabbit* Warne.

SENDAK, Maurice (1970) *Where the Wild Things Are* Picture Puffin.

SERRAILLIER, Ian (1960) *The Silver Sword* Puffin.

SEUSS, Dr (1961) *The Cat in the Hat* Beginner Books Collins.

SEUSS, Dr (1961) *The Cat in the Hat Comes Back* Beginner Books Collins.

SEUSS, Dr (1962) *Green Eggs and Ham* Beginner Books Collins.

Stithians School (1986) *Domesday Anniversary* Stithians School, Cornwall. Occasional Publication.

STYLES, Morag (1985) *I Like That Stuff* Cambridge University Press.

STYLES, Morag (1987) *You'll Love This Stuff* Cambridge University Press.

WATANABE, S (1981) *How Do I Put It On* Picture Puffin.

WATANABE, S (1986) *How Do I Put It On* Bodley Head. Editions in Bengali, Punjabi, Gujarati, Hindi, Vietnamese & Urdu.

WELLS, Rosemary (1978) *Noisy Norah* Picture Lions.

WHITE, E B (1963) *Charlotte's Web* Puffin. Also Lythway Large Print Books, Chivers Press 1986. (Hamish Hamilton 1952. Macmillan Education 1981.)

WILLIS, J & CHAMBERLAIN, M (1984) *The Tale of Mucky Mabel* Andersen Press. Also Sparrow Books 1985.

(1978) *Miss Priscilla's Secret* Warne.

Contributors

Linda Ashworth has taught infant children for many years. Until recently she was in charge of the infant department at Clifford Bridge School, Coventry. She has a longstanding interest in language and reading which is reflected in the articles she writes.

Myra Barrs has been associated with NATE for many years. She has a particular interest in children as writers and has published widely. She is currently the Warden of the Centre for Language in Primary Education in Inner London.

Henrietta Dombey was the first Chair of NATE from a background of Primary teaching, mainly in Inner London. Now she teaches in the Department of Primary Education at Brighton Polytechnic on both initial and in-service courses, with a special focus on early literacy.

Carol Fox is Senior Lecturer at Brighton Polytechnic. Her research into the narrative and literary competences of young children was carried out at Newcastle upon Tyne Polytechnic as part of a Language in Schools project directed by the late Dr K. Yerrill. A long-standing member of NATE, she is interested in the rich possibilities offered by children's oral story-telling for their personal, social, cognitive and linguistic development.

Gillian Lathey has spent ten years as a class teacher in an open-plan, vertically grouped infants school in London. She has a particular interest in young children as writers and is now working as an advisory teacher for language and literacy.

Colin Mills was, until recently, Senior Lecturer at Worcester College of Higher Education, where he taught language and literacy on initial training and in-service courses. He is now Lecturer at the University of Exeter. His research interests are in the social and cultural aspects of children's reading. He reviews children's books and is the editor, with Margaret Meek, of *Language and Literacy in the Primary School* (Falmer Press, 1988).

Shirley Paice has been teaching Primary School children in Essex for nearly twenty years. She has recently been appointed as Head of Epping County Infants school. She is committed to helping children to learn to read through exposure to a wide range of books, and is extremely concerned about the poor quality of many of the information books available for young children.

Deirdre Pettitt was an Infant teacher in Norfolk for several years. She was seconded to the University of East Anglia to be part of the Early Years Sector, involved in initial training and INSET. Her research interests have included writing from 4-9 and the use of mathematical games in the infant school. She is currently a lecturer in Primary Education at the University of Durham.

Sandra Smidt has taught for many years in inner city schools in both Manchester and London. Since 1980 she has been head of William Patten Infants School in Hackney, London. She is very interested in language learning, particularly that of bilingual and bidialectal children.

Anne Thomas taught in a number of Primary schools for thirteen years before becoming involved in in-service education. She is interested in all aspects of children's language development and is now a Senior Lecturer at the Centre for Language in Primary Education in Inner London.

David Thompson is deputy head in a small First School. He is particularly interested in poetry, children writing and the role of language throughout the Primary curriculum.

Linnea Timson has worked in Primary education for many years. She has a specific interest in language and literature in education, and is now Senior Lecturer at the Cornwall Education Centre, College of St Mark and St John.

Viv Wilson teaches at Hungerford Infants school. She has considerable experience of team teaching and a particular interest in the Arts and education.

Acknowledgements

Barrie Wade for permission to re-produce the leaflet *Tell Me A Story.*

The Times Educational Supplement for permission to reprint *Blanks in Teaching* by Myra Barrs (© *Times* Newspapers Ltd. 1984).

English in Education 21:2 (Summer 1987) for Henrietta Dombey's article 'Reading for Real from the Start'.

Cover photograph by Sue Smedley.

Particular thanks are due to Pat Barrett and Myra Barrs, who read this document at an earlier stage and offered helpful suggestions.

National Association for the Teaching of English

WHAT DOES IT MEAN TO YOU?

Why not join NATE now and enjoy the full benefits of membership.
You gain:

1   A professional subject association to represent your views on every aspect of English teaching.
2   Three copies annually of English in Education and the English Magazine to keep you up to date with news, reviews, opinion and debate.
3   Three copies annually of the NATE Newsletter: an informal round-up of what's happening where amongst NATE branches, and who does what elsewhere, together with some cryptic labour-saving reviews of what's new in print.
4   Free NATE publications on matters of concern to all English teachers.
5   Reduced prices for an expanding list of NATE publications.
6   Local branch membership and a share in local activities if you wish.
7   Attendance at the Annual Course and Conference at the reduced rate for NATE members.

Apply for membership now.

Simply write for an application form to:
NATE
Birley School Annexe, Fox Lane
Frecheville, Sheffield S12 4WY

OTHER BOOKS AVAILABLE FROM NATE

Children Reading to Their Teachers

This short book focuses on one of the commonest activities in the primary school classroom. The authors (all members of NATE Primary committee at the time when the book was written) are concerned to suggest ways in which the experience of reading aloud to a teacher can be as positive as possible for children and as informative as possible for teachers. They use the insights of psycholinguists like Ken Goodman to show how, in practical ways, teachers can concentrate on children's developing strengths as readers and can help them to feel more in control of the reading process. There are helpful short sections on basic tactics, using miscue, choosing books and record keeping by Dan Taverner, Cliff Moon, Anne Baker, Stephen Parker and Vivien Horobin, and a fascinating extended analysis of a twenty minute reading session with one child by Anne Baker. The book is introduced by Jill Bennett.

NATE member £2.95
Non-members £3.95

Helping Your Child with Reading and Writing

This 12-page booklet from the NATE 0–11 Committee and Working Party is addressed to parents and gives practical advice on how they might best encourage their children's reading and writing at home. It is sold in multiple copies for school and LEA purchase and is available in Bengali, Punjabi, Gujarati and Urdu as well as English.

English £6.00 for 10; £50.00 for 100
Other languages £2.50 for 5; £20.00 for 50

| ISBN: | Bengali | 0 901291 12 9 | Gujarati | 0 901291 14 5 |
| | Punjabi | 0 901291 13 7 | Urdu | 0 901291 15 3 |

Exploring Poetry 5-8

Jan Balaam & Brian Merrick

The book grew out of two years shared work in Jan Balaam's classroom. It began with the writers' belief that children should regularly hear a wide variety of poems – and also experience poetry for themselves through reading, speaking, dancing, music-making, drama or painting.

The authors describe the various ways in which they have introduced poems to young children and the range of activities they have used as a context in which to bring children closer to the poems. The book constitutes a workable poetry programme for the early school years. It includes many poems, detailed suggestions that will be especially useful to the more hesitant teacher and comprehensive booklists. Brian Merrick's full-page photographs of the class at work catch the children's enthusiastic involvement.

NATE members £7.25
Non-members £7.95

ISBN 0 901291 02 1

This book is a most valuable one for teachers working in the early years of primary schooling. Not only does it offer poems of real quality, but there are numerous well illustrated and fully documented outlines showing how to conduct sessions which will seize and stimulate young children's imagination and pleasure. Really good workable ideas are a precious commodity for busy teachers. This book is brimful of them. Indeed there is no longer any excuse for poetry being regarded as a dreary subject because enjoyment is on every page.
– Ted Wragg

A long overdue consideration of poetry usage for the first school and has a vitality which should inspire all who read it . . . *Exploring Poetry: 5-8* has that essential quality of being very readable as well as reassuring, listing ideas and approaches which have been common practice in the best of schools for some time (and on the best of teacher training courses!); there are also enough suggestions to ensure that many will be new and worth trying, whilst others which are already known may be further explored.
– Trevor Harvey: *Bookquest*